take five

one hundred meditations to de-stress your days

joseph m. champlin

take five

one hundred meditations to de-stress your days

SORIN BOOKS Notre Dame, Indiana

Imprimatur: Most Reverend Thomas J. Costello, D.D.
Vicar General, Diocese of Syracuse, New York
Nativity of the Lord, 2005

www.sorinbooks.com

ISBN-10 1-933495-04-9   ISBN-13 978-1-933495-04-0

Cover and text design by Brian C. Conley

Printed and bound in the United States of America.

Library of Congress Cataloging-in-Publication Data
Champlin, Joseph M.
  Take five : one hundred meditations to de-stress your day / Joseph Champlin.
      p. cm.
  ISBN-13: 978-1-933495-04-0 (pbk.)
  ISBN-10: 1-933495-04-9 (pbk.)
  1. Stress management--Religious aspects--Christianity--Meditations. 2. Stress (Psychology)--Religious aspects--Christianity--Meditations. I. Title.

BV4909.C38 2006
242'.4--dc22

                                        2006007841

Introduction

The murder of a physicist brought back memories to Robert Langdon, the central character in Dan Brown's novel, *Angels and Demons.* The murder evoked images of his own father's life and death. He recalled how as a young boy of six or seven, he heard his mother beg her spouse to "stop and smell the roses." The boy later remembered her words and bought his father a tiny, blown-glass rose for Christmas. He marveled at its beauty, "the way the sun caught it, throwing a rainbow of colors on the wall."

His father opened the gift at Christmas, pronounced it lovely, and kissed Robert on the forehead. "Let's find a safe spot for it," he said to his son. However, instead of putting the rose in the light, he carefully placed it on a high dusty shelf in the darkest corner of their living room. The boy was devastated. Several days later Robert took a stool, stood on it, retrieved the rose, and returned it to the store. He was further disillusioned when his father never noticed that the rose was missing.

Langdon also remembered the rainy and gray day of his father's funeral several years later, two days after his twelfth birthday. Gray-suited men walked around the house and many shook his hand. They all mumbled words like "cardiac" and "stress."

Radio Spots

In preparing rather recently to broadcast sixty-second inspirational spots over a local radio station, I sat with a dozen Clear Channel marketing and production people for an hour-long focus session. These were the topics for discussion: Who will be the audience? What are their concerns? How do we respond to them? They all strongly agreed that stress was the top challenge facing listeners. The group recommended a spiritual and religious but non-denominational and ecumenical approach.

The result was a series of daily radio spots: "Spiritual Suggestions to De-stress Your Day." The tag-on advertising line was: "You may have tried everything else, why not try God?" Ave Maria Press published the first hundred spots in 2004 as *Slow Down*, a small book of daily spiritual reflections. The second hundred, in a slightly different format, make up this book. The goal, however, is identical: meditations to de-stress your day.

Well-Founded Hope

These meditations should help diminish your anxious tensions and deepen your inner serenity, thus de-stressing your day. Here is why:

- Harvard cardiologist Dr. Herbert Benson, in a study funded by Transcendental Meditation advocates, found that people who practiced some form of spiritual reflection once or twice a day experienced a measurable reduction in the signs of stress, for example, blood pressure, heart beat, and sleep patterns.
- Jesus, two millennia earlier, must have known that. To his twelve excited apostles, returning after remarkably successful teaching and healing missions,

he simply said: "Come away by yourselves to a deserted place and rest awhile" (Mark 6:30–32).

- Jesus practiced what he preached. He often retired to deserted places and prayed, spent a night in communion with God, and regularly found time for prayer prior to crucial decisions and major events in his life.
- Jesus' ancestors did the same and offered similar advice. The prophet Isaiah urged the Chosen People: "By waiting and by calm you shall be saved, in quiet and in trust your strength lies" (Isaiah 30:15). The psalmist described his reflective prayer in this way: "I rise before dawn and cry out; I put my hope in your words" (Psalm 119:147).
- Followers of Christ have heeded his words and imitated his example.
- St. Francis of Assisi regularly interrupted his own busy preaching and teaching efforts for a month of prayer and reflection in an isolated location.
- Protestant leader and pastor David Wilkerson began to spend a lengthy time at night in prayer instead of watching television and found it changed his life.
- Mother Teresa of Calcutta insisted that her Missionaries of Charity pray for a lengthy period before and after their work with the poorest of the poor.
- A September 5, 2005, cover story in Newsweek deals with "Spirituality in America." The article begins by describing the increasingly popular prayer in which practitioners "find a quiet place to

sit with their eyes closed and surrender their minds to God." A survey revealed that 64 percent pray every day, 29 percent meditate daily; 40 percent feel their strongest connection to God when they are praying alone (pp. 48–49).

Many contemporary Americans have seemingly found that quiet prayer and meditation links them with the Divine Presence, the God of Peace. It no doubt calms them and—to at least some degree—de-stresses their days.

Proof in Practice

William is an ear, nose and throat specialist and his wife is an internist at a local hospital. In addition to a busy practice, this community-minded physician has been very active with the Salvation Army, even chairing its huge annual fund-raising luncheon. He and his wife, parents of three school-age children, began dance lessons a half-dozen years ago, enjoyed them, and now consider this their regular "couple time" away.

After more than two decades of conscientious and competent service in his field, William was confronted with a bitter medical malpractice suit. The case was complex, but the nearly six-year ordeal of lengthy depositions, withering accusations, and a painful trial left him devastated and disillusioned. Even though the jury by a swift and unanimous decision totally exonerated him, the wounds and scars remained.

Slow Down helped him to survive during this dark time in his life and to regain a better perspective about his profession. He keeps the book nearby, usually reading one or two entries between a morning full of surgeries and an afternoon occupied with patients at his office. Those brief interruptions seem to put his life into proper focus, reduce tensions and give him a certain peace.

Mary, a middle-aged wife, mother, and grandmother, recently completed her Ph.D. in educational administration and currently serves as principal of a public elementary school. A year or so ago, she began the *Slow Down* suggestion of daily reading and prayerful reflection. Her words describe the challenge and positive effects of that nearly everyday spiritual routine:

> I am working on the reflection process. It is helping me to identify areas I need to improve on, and I am seeing God's hands in so many ways. It is such a comfort to be increasingly aware of the Lord's care. The more carefully and thoughtfully I look, the more evidence I find. Very often it is through the kindness of people around me that God's presence comes through.
>
> Life is terribly busy, but the nights finally quiet down, and I even get some thinking time in the car. It's hard to believe that finding ten quiet minutes could be such a challenge!
>
> I've also found the more I pray, the more I look forward to quiet time to pray. That

seems to be a good thing. Getting quiet is difficult, but doable with effort!

Over twenty-five years ago, Tom, a business executive with an MBA from the Wharton School, assumed control of a company that designs, manufactures and installs equipment used in theaters and auditoriums. Today the company is a multi-million-dollar international business. Tom not only runs that firm, but also runs regularly for three to six miles at 5:00 each morning. He follows this jog by arranging his day and noting the resulting schedule in a hand-written planner. Two years ago he added another element to that regimen—a five minute meditation taken from *Slow Down*.

Tom has now been through the paperback three times and finds that this reflection process helps give him an inner peace. At the end of the refection and prayer, Tom selects a word or phrase from the *Slow Down* passage, which struck him and writes it in his planner. Later, at noon, in his office, the computer's software pops up before him a phrase: "God check." That prompts Tom to reread the word or words he had written earlier in his planner. "I may give it only eight seconds of reflection," he admits, "but that does bring me back to the morning's five-minute reflection. The book has helped me so much in reducing stress and deepening my spirituality that I've given it to a number of people, including several business associates."

Using This Book

After each meditation in this book, there is a spiritual suggestion, a scriptural thought for the day, and a reference to the biblical story from which that phrase has been taken. Depending upon the time available, readers could use these reflections in one of three ways:

1. Simply read the meditation, spiritual suggestion, and scriptural thought, then reflect upon the words for a minute or two. That would be about a five-minute exercise.
2. Follow the suggested process below for a more extended period of reflection.

A Meditation Process

1. Set aside a daily period for reflection. Aim for the same time each day.
2. Find a quiet space, where you probably will not be interrupted.
3. Get comfortable, but sit erect.
4. Breathe in deeply twice, then exhale. Repeat.
5. Breathe in a third time, and sense that you are inhaling God's goodness and light. Exhale evil and darkness.
6. Read the message. Perhaps, in some cases, read it a second time.
7. Move on to the spiritual suggestion and scriptural thought.
8. Spend the remaining moments reflecting upon the message, the suggestion, and the thought.
9. Before finishing, reread the scriptural thought.

10. During the day, try to occasionally recall a word or phrase from the scriptural thought and let it help de-stress you.

Use #1 or #2 above and also make this a regular occasion for reading the Bible. Simply look up the passage from which the scriptural thought is taken and prayerfully ponder that story or excerpt during your day.

These spiritual suggestions have emerged from my own lived experiences, "urban legends," a few presentations by others, and my own reading. May they bring you some good thoughts, healthy spiritual habits, and fewer stressful days.

FATHER JOSEPH CHAMPLIN
WARNERS, NEW YORK
FALL 2005

The Bright and Good, Dark and Bad within Us

One of our familiar street persons illustrates that we all have something dark and bright, good and bad within us. Blessed with a brilliant mind, the man is clear, cogent, and quite spiritual when the bright and the good dominate his life. But at moments when the dark and the bad take over, he becomes incoherent, vile, and even violent.

Last spring I walked by him as he sat on the sidewalk feeding the pigeons. He called out to me, but I pretended not to hear the man, wishing to avoid another unpleasant scene. He called again, and I reluctantly acknowledged him.

"What that patch on your head?" he said.

"I had a skin cancer which was surgically removed."

He responded: "I hope it turns out all right for you." The bright and good in him surfaced.

Spiritual Suggestion:

We need to respect others, even when their dark and bad external behavior annoys or otherwise disturbs us.

Scriptural Thought:

"Love your enemies, do good to those who hate you, bless those who curse you, pray for those who mistreat you."

Biblical Story:

A teaching on the love of enemies in Luke 6:27–36

DAY 2

Heroic Patriotism

Mike Christian grew up in a small town near Selma, Alabama, never wore shoes until he was thirteen, and at seventeen enlisted in the Navy. He became a Navy pilot and an officer, was shot down, captured, and spent about a half-dozen years in the harsh confinement of a Vietnamese prison cell.

While imprisoned, Mike wove an American flag out of his prison blue shirt and two gifts from home: a white handkerchief and a red scarf. Every afternoon at 4:00, he and several dozen other prisoners fastened the makeshift flag to the wall and recited the Pledge of Allegiance.

One day the guards discovered the shirt, confiscated it, and beat him badly that night. Several hours later, under a dim light, with his eyes half-shut from the beating, Mike made another flag so his companions would not lose hope.

Spiritual Suggestion:

The heroic and unselfish patriotism of a prisoner in Vietnam should inspire within us a similar love for others.

Scriptural Thought:

"For this is the message you have heard from the beginning: we should love one another . . . "

Biblical Story:

An exhortation to love in 1 John 3:11–18

Becoming Involved and Saving a Life

Joel Delaney, the physician's assistant at a local family practice office, was varnishing a porch that overlooks a small lake in Onondaga Park. Suddenly he heard children running up the street screaming for help. He jumped off the porch, ran to the lake, climbed over a railing and spotted a six-year-old boy submerged in the lake with his white shoes sticking up in the water. Delaney, thirty-two, said, "I was scared and at first panicked." But then his inner courage and medical training took over.

Joel jumped into the lake and pulled the boy out. The child wasn't breathing and had turned blue. Delaney began CPR. Shortly thereafter the youngster coughed up water and started breathing, with color returning to his face. The child's shaken grandmother declared: "God sent us a angel today. I will remember Mr. Delaney in my prayers and thank God for saving my grandson through him."

Spiritual Suggestion:

Getting involved at unlikely times can bring blessings to others, even saving their lives.

Scriptural Thought:

"Go in peace, may the God of Israel grant you what you have asked ... "

Biblical Story:

The prayer of Hannah and the birth of Samuel in 1 Samuel 1:1–28

DAY 4

Growing in Awareness through Dependency

Father Ron Lewinski had just finished the enormous task of constructing a multi-million-dollar church complex on the outskirts of Chicago. Soon afterwards, however, he tore his Achilles tendon while playing racquetball with a friend. The injury was painful and crippling; the healing process, long and burdensome. Someone had to drive him everywhere. To do anything always took longer. Dining in a restaurant with tables close together became an embarrassing challenge. Forced for weeks to navigate in a wheelchair, he became more sensitive to persons with disabilities.

He still limps a bit and climbing stairs hurts a little, but the priest is grateful for his greater awareness of people with similar disabilities that often last a lifetime.

Spiritual Suggestion:

When an injury or an illness leaves us at least temporarily dependent upon others, we can grow in our awareness of those with disabilities.

Scriptural Thought:

"You are the God of the lowly, the helper of the oppressed, the supporter of the weak, the protector of the forsaken, the savior of those without hope."

Biblical Story:

Judith's prayer and the deliverance of the Jews in Judith 8–13

Reflecting Every Day

Each morning Bishop Robert Morneau, a Wisconsin pastor, lecturer, and poet, goes down to the river, sits on a log, and reflects upon the previous day's events. This practice connects his experiences with God and makes them richer human events for him to mine.

Bishop Morneau also stresses the number 144. There are, he points out, that many ten-minute segments every day. Is it too much, he asks, to give two of the daily 144 segments over to our relationship with God? We could use them for praying, reading the Bible, or reflecting upon the divine presence in the previous day's life experiences. Those ten-minute reflections could fill us with peaceful gratitude and confidence—helping us praise God in our joys and turn to God in our sorrows.

Spiritual Suggestion:

Taking ten minutes once or twice a day can make our life experiences richer.

Scriptural Thought:

"Behold, I am the handmaid of the Lord. May it be done to me according to your word."

Biblical Story:

Gabriel's announcement to Mary in Luke 1:26–38

Day 6

Making the Right, Not Necessarily Popular, Decisions

Rick Carlisle took over as coach of the Detroit Pistons in the National Basketball Association and immediately turned the team around. Under his direction they enjoyed two successful seasons and even had the best record in their conference. But Joe Dumars, president of the Piston's basketball operations, fired Carlisle as soon as the season ended. Why did he take this surprising step?

Because, he said, there is more to coaching that simply winning games. Apparently Carlisle was abusive, caused friction, and aggravated his players, employees, and even the owners.

Dumars's decision was not a popular one, but he is at peace with it. He commented afterward: "I sleep at night when I have to make tough decisions. I'm not in the business of making popular decisions; I have to make right and wrong decisions. I felt at this time, that this was the right decision for us to make."

Spiritual Suggestion:

There can be peace within us when we make the right, even if not popular, decision.

Scriptural Thought:

"You have been told . . . , what is good, and what the Lord requires of you: Only to do the right and

to love goodness, and to walk humbly with your
God."

Biblical Story:

The prophet Micah tells his people what God expects of them in Micah 6:1–8

A Model Father

Lavar Arrington plays linebacker for the Washington Redskins and has been chosen for the ProBowl several times. This big, strapping, and fast football player looks to his father for inspiration. Arrington's dad was badly disabled by an accident in Vietnam. His son describes what happened and how his father inspired him. "I look up to my dad a great deal. He lost both his feet as well as a knee and a thigh on one leg. He uses two prosthetic legs and gets around better and is more active than some people who have both legs."

The talented football player also praises the virtues of his dad when he says, "I'm really proud of my father for being a man who my brothers and I can look up to and pattern ourselves after. He's always been a figure of stability, strength, and perseverance." A model father mirrors God, the perfect parent, and can inspire his children to follow his good example.

Spiritual Suggestion:

Good fathers, mirroring God who is the perfect parent, inspire their children to imitate them.

Scriptural Thought:

"God put Abraham to the test. 'Abraham!' 'Ready!' he replied . . ." "I know now how devoted you are to God, since you did not withhold from me your beloved son."

Biblical Story:

Abraham with his son Isaac in Genesis 22:1–19

Praying Often Each Day

A man originally from Pakistan staffs the Business Centre of the Marriott Hotel near Toronto's International Airport. As he was tending to the message I was faxing home, this well-groomed, middle-aged clerk volunteered that he was a Muslim. He also mentioned that when he prays during work hours, customers seem to wait with patience and respect. "Five times a day, right?" I commented, remembering that this is the Muslim tradition.

"Oh yes," he replied, his face brightening into a smile. He then rushed over to a cupboard and opened it up to display the special prayer rug upon which he kneels, with forehead touching the floor and his body turned east, toward Mecca. During daytime, the prayer interval is brief, about three minutes, but at night this adoration of God lasts nearly a half-hour.

Spiritual Suggestion:

The example of faithful Muslims who kneel for prayer five times daily should impress us in many ways.

Scriptural Thought:

"You shall love the Lord, your God, with all your heart, with all your soul, and with all your mind."

Biblical Story:

Jesus' initial response to the inquiry, "Which is the greatest commandment?" in Matthew 22:34–40

DAY 9

Holiday Sadness and Comfort

Holiday seasons can be particularly painful for those who have suffered a personal loss—for example, the death of one we deeply loved, a divorce, or sudden unemployment. Novelist Nicholas Sparks captures that sorrow and also some compensating comfort in his novel *The Guardian*.

Jules, a widow at only twenty-five, had lost her wonderful husband to a brain tumor just months earlier. On Christmas Eve, a young man knocked on the door, then dropped off a box for her with a gift and a message inside. The gift was a puppy, and a note was from her deceased spouse who had arranged this present and communication prior to his death.

The letter explained the gift and ended: "Don't worry. From wherever I am, I'll watch out for you. I'll be your guardian angel, sweetheart. You can count on me to keep you safe. I love you."

Spiritual Suggestion:

When grieving over a loss, especially during the holiday season, connecting with those we love can comfort us.

Scriptural Thought:

"God will wipe away every tear from their eyes, and there shall be no more death or mourning, wailing or pain, for the old order has passed away."

Biblical Story:

The new heaven and the new earth in Revelation 21:1–8

Someone to Watch over Me

Soprano Lee Merrill, wife and mother of two children from Springfield, Ohio, beautifully sang Gershwin's lovely ballad, "Someone to Watch Over Me" at a Symphony Pops Concert. I hear the hope for fulfillment of that dream many times when I ask future brides why they wish to marry the man of their dreams. Almost all reply in this way: "He is my best friend. I can simply be myself in his presence. I know he will always be there for me."

The grooms usually reply: "Everything she said I agree with." Is that a prelude to "Yes, dear?"

My best friend who will always be there for me sounds very much like "Someone to Watch Over Me." While that dream or ideal is noble and healthy, couples need to realize that only God perfectly watches over us, and only God can be there for me at any moment and on all occasions.

Spiritual Suggestion:

While we look for the ideal someone to watch over us, only God can perfectly do so.

Scriptural Thought:

"Then Isaac took Rebekah into his tent; he married her, and thus she became his wife. In his love for her, Isaac found solace after the death of his mother Sarah."

Biblical Story:

Isaac and Rebekah in Genesis 24

Day 11

Coincidences

The son of a local optometrist graduated from West Point and now serves as an army officer in Iraq. His parents' daily concern about the safety of their young man is understandably intense and constant.

Several weeks ago, the optometrist and his wife decided to head to the slopes for a day of skiing. Just before starting the car, the father remembered he hadn't packed his ski boots. He ran to get them and, just inside the door, heard the phone ringing. It was their son calling from Iraq, the first they had heard from him in six months. After assuring them he was fine in every way, they talked for more than a half-hour.

Was the father's return to the house a mere fluke or a divine coincidence? Either way, people with faith will view it as a sign of God's loving presence in our midst.

Spiritual Suggestion:

View with faith positive coincidences as manifestations of God's loving kindness toward us.

Scriptural Thought:

"The Lord was not in the wind, the earthquake or the fire but in a tiny whispering sound."

Biblical Story:

Elijah and God's message in 1 Kings 19:1–18

The Wonder of a Baby

At the baptism of a baby, I always pose this question to the proud parents: "How, Dad and Mom, did you feel when this little infant came into the world?" The answers, expressed in different ways, communicate an identical attitude: "I felt joy," "love," "overwhelmed," "grateful," "ecstatic," "in awe." The father of a ten pound six ounce girl said he felt very proud; the mother of course felt relieved.

One obstetrician observed that despite delivering thousands of babies, he never got over the miracle, the wonder of it all.

God is present in the parents' self-giving that leads to conception. And it is God's creative presence that gives life, the soul, to a baby. Our sense of awe, wonder, and miracle is, therefore, not surprising at all.

Spiritual Suggestion:

We need to stand in awe before the conception and birth of a baby, realizing that is a self-giving, collaborative effort involving God and the parents.

Scriptural Thought:

"O Lord, my God, you are great indeed!"

Biblical Story:

Praise of God the Creator in Psalm 104

DAY 13

Self-Satisfaction through Self-Discipline

There is great self-satisfaction when we accomplish something significant through a period of challenging self-discipline.

- When I finished the Ottawa Marathon in my mid-fifties alive and under four hours, I experienced a great sense of accomplishment. But running those 26 miles and 265 yards was possible only because of serious training for two months.
- People who have lost unhealthy weight through special diets and regular exercise feel better and are proud of themselves and that they successfully followed a regimen of such self-discipline.
- When U.S. Marine recruits complete the intense three months of boot camp at Parris Island, South Carolina, they will be smartly disciplined, physically fit, and trained in the basics. They will also likely have a great sense of satisfaction in a job well done.

Spiritual Suggestion:

Recognize the great satisfaction that comes to us when we accomplish something through a period of challenging self-discipline.

Scriptural Thought:

"Whoever wishes to come after me must deny himself, take up his cross, and follow me."

Biblical Story:

Requirements of discipleship in Matthew 16:24–28

Keeping Relationships Alive by Time Away

The man returning home to Kansas City from a business trip has been married fifteen years and is the father of two boys. He and his wife met as Peace Corps volunteers working in Costa Rica. They eventually fell in love and returned to the United States for employment here. While the two boys are the light of their lives, the man worries about how well he and his wife are relating. The couple have never left the boys since their birth; they have not gone out, just the two of them ever, not even for dinner, much less for an overnight or a weekend. He sees that as a weakness, almost a danger, something that needs to be changed. They will, he judges, be better parents if their own relationship is strong, deep, and flourishing.

Spiritual Suggestion:

All of us, including parents, need to get away occasionally to strengthen and deepen our relationships.

Scriptural Thought:

"Come away by yourselves to a deserted place and rest awhile."

Biblical Story:

The excited disciples return from successful teaching and healing missions in Mark 6:30–33

Day 15

Alzheimer's Disease

A month ago I was sitting in the office helping an engaged couple prepare for marriage when my private phone rang. The caller, a dear friend and family member, had telephoned across the country simply to see how I was doing. We chatted for a moment and I returned to the couple. Five minutes later the phone rang again. It was the same man, asking the same question and my heart sank.

I knew by this incident that my friend's short-term memory had deteriorated. But this incident pointed to a more rapid decline and the onset of Alzheimer's disease. Experts in the field confirmed that these symptoms indicated he had reached the middle stages of this illness. I now joined those thousands of people who in various ways care for people with such a difficult disease. It was clear that patience, wisdom, and love would be required.

Spiritual Suggestion:

Caregivers need patience, wisdom, and love in their encounters with those suffering from Alzheimer's disease and other forms of dementia.

Scriptural Thought:

"Do not fear or lose heart . . . .Trust in the Lord, your God, and you will be found firm."

Biblical Story:

The prophet reassures a frightened King Jehoshaphat in 2 Chronicles 20:1–30

Generous Hearts

As part of his training, the young man studying in the United States to become a priest spent three weeks working in a poor section of Brazil. He expected to share his abundance with the impoverished people there. Instead he found himself enriched by their generosity.

A family invited the student and his colleagues for lunch. They had prepared a huge feast, including cans of soda pop, but would not eat until their guests had finished. Later the young man learned that this family could not afford soft drinks for themselves.

A nine-year-old girl, cute as a button, spent several days with these students. She always wore the same clothes, together with a necklace sporting a paper thin cross on it. When he was leaving to return home, she took the necklace off and gave it to him as a reminder of his short time with her people. The young man is likely to become a more generous priest because of their generous hearts.

Spiritual Suggestion:

The generous hearts of people who are poor can touch the hearts of those who have abundance.

Scriptural Thought:

"Do not worry about tomorrow; tomorrow will take care of itself." "Seek first the Kingdom of God . . . and all these things will be given you besides."

Biblical Story:

Dependence upon God in Matthew 6:25–34

DAY 17

Our Uniqueness

When Pope John Paul II visited Colorado some time ago, he spent a day resting at St. Malo's Retreat House. This conference center lies at the base of Mt. Meeker in the Rocky Mountains. Residents point out to visitors how unique are the rock formations to be viewed while driving through this glorious region. Every one is different; no two are the same.

We human beings are similar to these natural wonders. Each one of us is likewise unique; no two persons are absolutely identical; everyone is totally different. The Hebrew scriptures teach that truth. God calls each of us by name, tells every one of us that we are glorious, precious, and divinely loved.

The Christian scriptures speak the same message. God reminds us that all the hairs of our head are numbered. Recognizing that we are so unique and special in God's sight should help us let our worries go.

Spiritual Suggestion:

I need to remember that God calls me by name, knows who I am, and loves me in a unique way.

Scriptural Thought:

"Yet, O Lord, you are our father; we are the clay and you the potter."

Biblical Story:

We are the work of God's hands in Isaiah 64:1–11

Living the Wedding Vows

The couple stood before the altar pledging to take and love each other for better, for worse, for richer, for poorer, in good times and in bad, until death do they part. Now a half-century later, they are living out those vows in ways which neither, of course, could have imagined.

Five years ago, an eye specialist told the husband: "Friend, you are legally blind through macular degeneration." This would be devastating for anyone. But for a man whose professional life has centered on reading, viewing films, and writing, this partial blindness has been particularly painful. His greatest frustration: the inability to read. The second: the inability to drive. His wife has been his eyes: reading newspapers, mail, and menus as well as driving their car.

Her hearing has now deteriorated, and he has become her ears.

Spiritual Suggestion:

Living the wedding vows is quite different from making them.

Scriptural Thought:

"This is why a man leaves his father and mother and clings to his wife, and the two of them become one body."

Biblical Story:

Creation of woman in Genesis 2:15–25

Day 19

Wise Leadership

General Ulysses Grant, a West Point graduate, had an addiction to alcohol that caused him to resign from the army in 1850. Once the Civil War started, however, he was pressed back into service and did so with resounding success. When rumors spread that his drinking problem had resurfaced, President Abraham Lincoln, with typical wisdom, sent someone to find out the facts about the situation.

Reports indicated that while indeed Grant had an addiction to alcohol, it did not seem to interfere with his responsibilities as a general. Lincoln remarked that if he knew the brand of whiskey Grant was using, he would immediately buy a bottle and send it to all of his generals.

Spiritual Suggestion:

Leaders would do well to pray for the kind of wisdom and leadership that Abraham Lincoln displayed on many occasions.

Scriptural Thought:

"Give your servant, therefore, an understanding heart to judge your people and to distinguish right from wrong."

Biblical Story:

The wisdom of Solomon in 1 Kings 3

Through Adversity to Gratitude

Danielle Green played basketball at the University of Notre Dame. She later became a soldier and married. Danielle lost her wedding ring while on guard duty at the top of a Baghdad police station. A rocket-propelled grenade blew off her left hand and with it, of course, the wedding band. Despite going through seven surgeries and endless therapy, Danielle has a great spirit of gratitude.

"I am really thankful . . . I probably shouldn't be here, but I am."

She goes on to say: "I appreciate what I have now. I don't think about what I don't have. Even our have-nots have more than the Iraqi civilians have. I have a deeper understanding and appreciation for life in America. It makes me more thankful."

Spiritual Suggestion:

Do serious adversities in life, like crippling injuries or critical illnesses, make me more grateful for what I have?

Scriptural Thought:

"Naked I come forth from my mother's womb, and naked shall I go back again. The Lord gave and the Lord has taken away; blessed be the name of the Lord!"

Biblical Story:

The wealthy and pious Job during his trial in Job 1

Day 21

Self-Giving

The young man had been raised a Catholic and went to Catholic schools. Upon graduation he became a very successful salesman, working in two different fields. The fellow's life, in his words, revolved around three things: making a lot of money, drinking a lot, and womanizing. After a period of time, however, he felt restless. There were no big problems, but he said to himself: "My whole life is centered on me, getting what I want, doing what I desire." He sensed a certain emptiness in his heart.

Recognizing that he had some emotional problems, drank too much, and was sexually irresponsible, the man turned to prayer and asked God for help.

Now, ten years later, after therapy, regular AA meetings, and living a chaste life, he is about to embark upon a career that will require constant self-giving but promises a contented heart.

Spiritual Suggestion:

The self-giving heart is content; the self-seeking heart is restless.

Scriptural Thought:

"So Jacob served seven years for Rachel, yet they seemed to him but a few days because of his love for her."

Biblical Story:

The marriage of Jacob to Leah and Rachel in Genesis 29:1–30

Misguided Parents

Over the past dozen years, I have been surprised and dismayed on several occasions by parents who have given teenage children too much freedom. These were and are basically good dads and moms. However, to my shock, they have permitted and even supported certain actions that, it seems to me, are disasters waiting to happen. The incidents involve unchaperoned night parties for high school students where liquor is served. For one thing, serving alcohol to minors is illegal in most states, and the potential disasters are enormous. How often do we hear of fatal accidents caused by teenagers driving under the influence?

Putting adolescents in such situations is asking too much of them. And this places heavy burdens on those other fathers and mothers who judge, correctly, that unchaperoned parties with liquor for teenagers is bad and misguided parenting.

Spiritual Suggestions:

Parents who give children too much freedom open the doors to disaster.

Scriptural Thought:

"Blessed be the Lord, the God of Israel, who made heaven and earth, for having given King David a wise son of intelligence and understanding, who will build a house for the Lord ... "

Biblical Story:

Solomon as the Builder of the Temple in 2 Chronicles 1–6

Trusting in God

When John XXIII became pope, he was nearly eighty, but he soon won the world over with his warmth, humor, and wisdom. He convened the Second Vatican Council in the 1960s, calling all Roman Catholic bishops of the world together. Why did he do this? In his words: "To open the windows and let some fresh air into the Church." When asked how many people work at the Vatican, Pope John XXIII once responded: "About half of them!"

At the end of each day, this elderly spiritual leader retired to his chapel for prayer. There were many burdens on his shoulders: wars, the Vatican Council, and the care of millions of Catholics worldwide. One would think he prayed for hours. Quite the contrary: He knelt down and simply said: "Lord, it's your Church and I am going to bed."

Spiritual Suggestion:

Placing our work in God's hands can reduce our worry and stress.

Scriptural Thought:

"Take care you remain tranquil and do not fear."

Biblical Story:

Isaiah's prophecy to King Ahaz about the birth of Immanuel in Isaiah 7:1–16

Pondering the Negative and Ignoring the Positive

I recently gave seven hour-long lectures to around one hundred priests in a neighboring area. They seemed to respond quite positively to my presentations, and afterwards a few individual comments were very praiseworthy of my remarks. A week later I received a survey of the written evaluations. Participants rated the lectures in this way: forty-six "very favorable," fourteen "favorable," and one "disappointing." There were written comments, nearly all positive, including "best ever," "outstanding," "very refreshing." But there were two negatives: "No great depth" and "very disappointing."

What do you think I dwelled upon afterward? The two negatives of course! We have an almost innate tendency in our lives to ponder the negatives and ignore the positives.

Spiritual Suggestion:

We have an unfortunate tendency to dwell on a single negative comment and ignore the many positive remarks.

Scriptural Thought:

"A prophet is not without honor except in his native place and in his own house."

Biblical Story:

Rejection of Jesus at Nazareth in Matthew 13:54–58

DAY 25

God's Presence and Protection

I recently baptized a baby whose father has been deployed in Iraq and is not scheduled to return home for six months. The infant's grandmother told me that she had purchased a religious card, attached it to a photo of the mother and baby, laminated the combined materials and sent it to the father in Iraq. The soldier stuck the prayer and photos in the felt lining of his helmet.

Sometime later an insurgent shot him in the head and the helmet saved his life. Where did the bullet hit, leaving a dent in the helmet? Precisely at the spot where the prayer card had been placed. He and his family consider this not as a mere coincidence, but as a sign of God's loving presence and protection.

Faith enables one to look beyond and see God's hand in such events.

Spiritual Suggestion:

Faith enables us see God's loving presence and protection in our lives.

Scriptural Thought:

"This is the sign that I am giving for all ages to come, of the covenant between me and you and every living creature with you: I set my bow in the clouds. . . . As the bow appears in the clouds, I will see it and recall the everlasting covenant that I have established between God and all living beings . . ."

Biblical Story:

Noah and the Ark in Genesis 9:8–17

Just Being

On the Amtrak train to Toronto, we passed high over a fairly substantial river or canal. Looking down from the coach windows, I saw several people sitting on a well-kept grassy area next to the water. They weren't really doing anything. They weren't eating around a picnic table, playing cards, or monitoring a group of children. They were just sitting there, presumably marveling at the beautiful day, enjoying the serenity that flowing water can give to our inner selves and appreciating one another's company.

In our society and culture, just being, just sitting and absorbing the beauty of life and relationships isn't easy. There is the strong compulsion that we all seem to possess for pure action, to be doing something. But the Bible says: "Be still and know that I am God." That cluster of people sitting by the river's edge appeared—at least to my hopeful eyes—to be following that divine directive.

Spiritual Suggestion:

There are times when it is profitable just to *be* for a few moments and resist the need to *do* something that is outwardly productive.

Scriptural Thought:

"Mary kept all these things, reflecting on them in her heart."

Biblical Story:

The shepherds visit Mary and the child in Luke 2: 15–20

A Story of Faith and Love

A married couple living in the Midwest combined the wife's strong faith in the Lord with her husband's apparent lack of belief in God. She believed but, unable to drive, seldom attended church. Instead, the Bible and religious television programs fed her faith. He struggled to believe at all.

Late in life, the wife suffered from dementia. People gave her a book, but she frequently placed it in the oven. She often lost her purse. Still, the woman constantly held a Bible and with great affection gently stroked it. In those later days, the husband deeply regretted not having driven her to church while she was healthier.

After his wife's death, he took her Bible and read it from cover to cover.

Spiritual Suggestion:

Responding late to God's nudges is better than never doing it at all.

Scriptural Thought:

"I knew that you are a gracious and merciful God, slow to anger, rich in clemency, loathe to punish."

Biblical Story:

Jonah and the whale in Jonah 1–4

DAY 28

Remembering

In early November, many Canadians wear circular red poppies on their lapels, blouses, or shirts. They are celebrating Remembrance Day—we call it Veterans Day—as they honor the memory of those in the armed forces who have served their country. The poppies bring to mind that poem "In Flanders Field," composed during World War I and memorized by many of our own students in their early school years. During these days of terrorism, the words still ring true.

In Flanders fields the poppies blow
Between the crosses, row on row,
That mark our place; and in the sky
The larks, still bravely singing, fly
Scarce heard amid the guns below.
We are the Dead. Short days ago
We lived, felt dawn, saw sunset glow,
Loved and were loved, and now we lie
In Flanders fields.
Take up our quarrel with the foe:
To you from failing hands we throw
The torch; be yours to hold it high.
If ye break faith with us who die
We shall not sleep, though poppies grow
In Flanders fields.

COLONEL JOHN McCRAE, M.D.

DAY 28 (continued)

Spiritual Suggestion:

As Canadians observe Remembrance Day by wearing a red poppy in memory of those who have served their nation in the armed forces, we too do well to remember with prayer and gratitude those who give their lives for this country and our freedom.

Scriptural Thought:

"If only I had died instead of you, Absalom, my son, my son!"

Biblical Story:

David and Absalom in 2 Samuel 18:1–32; 19:1

The Poor Helping the Poor

An already impoverished nation, Jamaica suffered further hardships from recent hurricanes. Several young children on that troubled island ran down the mountain to their church's pastor. They told him in nervous excitement: "Our mother is dying; she doesn't want to live anymore." He followed them back to the shack that is their home and found the children's mother sitting on a bench weeping. She was deeply depressed over having no food for her children.

Later the pastor returned with a week's supply of beans and rice for the family. When he checked on the family several days later, he found that this kind and generous woman had given half of his donated food to a neighbor woman who was equally impoverished and discouraged.

Spiritual Suggestion:

The generous spirit of many people, even those without enough for themselves, can surprise and inspire us.

Scriptural Thought:

"Blessed are the poor in spirit, for theirs is the kingdom of heaven."

Biblical Story:

The Beatitudes in Matthew 5:1–12

DAY 30

Being Lost, Confused, and Vulnerable

I recently drove to Strong Memorial Hospital in Rochester to visit a friend having serious surgery there. It was unfamiliar territory, and the directions to the place a bit complicated. Fortunately those big H signs at every junction led me right to the front entrance of the huge complex. However, getting from the massive parking garage to the hospital, to the right room, and back again was even more confusing. Because of that, I kept asking people for guidance.

I felt very vulnerable at those moments when I had to ask for help. I was lost or confused, and totally dependent upon others. I realized later that this experience paralleled my relationship with God, or at least what it often is or should be—vulnerable, lost, confused, and totally dependent upon a loving God for guidance.

Spiritual Suggestion:

Times when we are lost, confused, or vulnerable and helped by others can remind us of our own relationship with God.

Scriptural Thought:

"My Lord, our King, you alone are God. Help me, who am alone and have no help but you . . . "

Biblical Story:

Queen Esther saves God's people in Esther 3–7

Growing Humility: Part 1

The following thought from the Book of Sirach is worth taping to a bathroom mirror or refrigerator door. It states, "Conduct your affairs with humility, and you will be loved more than a giver of gifts." For the next three days, we will suggest ways you can grow in humility or become more humble.

The first step is to realize that everything is a gift, a gift ultimately from God. We readily recognize that truth in the case of an infant in the womb, the birth of a baby, or a tiny child at the mother's breast. As we grow older and more self-reliant, we can forget our dependency and that life is pure gift. But to remind us of our gifts, we need only to gaze at a magnificent sunset, rejoice over the fall foliage, or reflect upon the air we breathe.

Spiritual Suggestion:

To recognize that everything is a gift, ultimately from God, is the first step to becoming more humble.

Scriptural Thought:

"Conduct your affairs with humility, and you will be loved more than a giver of gifts."

Biblical Story:

A treatise on humility in Sirach 3:17–28

Day 32

Growing Humility: Part II

The Bible says: "Conduct your affairs with humility and you will be loved more than a giver of gifts." Yesterday we described a first step for growing in humility or becoming more humble: Recognize that everything is a gift, ultimately from God. For today, here is a second step in that process: realize that we are unique creations of God.

In the scriptures, God reminds us of that truth by saying: "I have called you by name . . . .you are glorious and precious and I love you" (Is 43:1,4). "Even the hairs of your head have all been counted" (Lk 12:7). Our experience tells us that as well: No one else has my fingerprints or my DNA. Each one of us is indeed a unique creation of God.

Spiritual Suggestion:

To realize that we are unique creations of God is the second step to becoming more humble.

Scriptural Thought:

"God looked at everything he had made, and he found it very good."

Biblical Story:

The first story of creation in Genesis 1

Growing Humility: Part III

Once again, the Bible states: "Conduct your affairs with humility and you will be loved more than a giver of gifts." We have been describing steps on how to grow in humility or become more humble: Step One: recognize that everything is a gift, ultimately from God. Step Two: realize that you are a unique creation of God. Today, Step Three: respect the special gifts of others.

We have our own unique gifts, but others have theirs as well. I am always impressed with healthcare workers who have talents for serving difficult patients and love their work. Not everyone has those gifts and that love. Respecting the gifts of others causes us to rejoice in their successes and lament with them their failures.

Spiritual Suggestion:

Respect the unique gifts which others possess.

Scriptural Thought:

"The community of believers was of one heart and mind . . . they had everything in common. . . . There was no needy person among them."

Biblical Story:

Unity and sharing among the first Christians in Acts 4:32–35

Selfishness

I left a conference in New Orleans just ahead of Hurricane Ivan. However, the initial evacuation order had been given in the morning and the major highways were already clogged with bumper-to-bumper traffic. The trip from downtown to the airport normally takes about thirty minutes but that day we spent three and one-half hours creeping along to catch a plane. Many people's patience eventually wears thin in such situations.

The highway had a large shoulder, wide enough for a car. Occasionally an aggressive driver would race by and, then, some way ahead, seek to push into the line of slowly moving vehicles. Some charitable soul would let the driver in. Many others, observing the event, got very annoyed, presuming the first driver acted out of pure selfishness. Someone remarked: "That's how road rage happens."

Spiritual Suggestion:

Selfishness and rushing to judgment can lead to harmful reactions and often serious injury.

Scriptural Thought:

"Watch and pray that you may not undergo the test. The spirit is willing, but the flesh is weak."

Biblical Story:

Weakness of Peter and the others in the garden in Matthew 26:36–46

An Unselfish Deed

I was driving out in the country immediately after a moderately heavy thunderstorm. As I made my way through a village and up a slight hill leading out of that rural hamlet, I saw that a car had stopped at the top of the incline. I came to a halt, then watched an older man get out of the car, walk behind it, pick up a good size fallen branch, and throw it to the side of the road.

He didn't need to do that. The man had already driven around or over the large branch. But someone else, like myself, would soon follow and encounter the branch. I was impressed and inspired by this man's unnecessary but thoughtful gesture. Good deeds have that effect. They can motivate us to go forward and do likewise.

Spiritual Suggestion:

> The thoughtful deed of another can inspire us to do the same.

Scriptural Thought:

> *"You are the light of the world."*

Biblical Story:

> Our call to be salt and light in Matthew 5:13–16

Day 36

Frustration and Worry, Relief and Joy

We flew to Philadelphia early on the day after a winter storm had closed eastern seaboard airports. US Air cancelled the connecting flight to our final destination. No confirmed space was available until the next night. We could, however, standby for a flight that evening. Only 25 percent of the airport work force showed up because of the storm, resulting in very long lines and overtaxed agents. A day of worrisome waiting ended in frustration when there was no room for us on the evening plane.

We found a nearby motel, slept several hours, and then rushed to the airport as standbys for an early morning flight. The cloud now lifted. Airline personnel at the gate found seats for us. Great relief and joy flooded over me as I buckled up for the trip south, a relief and joy growing out of the prior day's adversity and worry.

Spiritual Suggestion:

Great relief and joy sometimes follows frustration and worry.

Scriptural Thought:

"Rejoice in the Lord always. I shall say it again: rejoice! Your kindness should be known to all. The Lord is near. Have no anxiety at all . . . .Then the peace of God that surpasses all understanding will guard your hearts and minds . . . "

Biblical Story:

An exhortation on joy and peace in Philippians 4:4–9

Questions about Heaven

Alice Sebold's first novel, *The Lovely Bones,* topped the *New York Times* bestseller list for some weeks. Her story begins with a gripping account of the violent rape and murder of fourteen-year-old Susie Salmon. The rest of the novel describes Susie in heaven over a period of years, observing the lives of her parents, family, friends, and Mr. Harvey who murdered her. The intriguing tale raises many worthwhile questions about the nature of heaven:

- Does heaven exist?
- What is life like there?
- Are people in heaven aware of those still on earth?
- Do they help us?
- Do they sometimes appear to us?
- Should we ask for their assistance?

Spiritual Suggestion:

Read *The Lovely Bones* and ponder some worthwhile questions about the nature of heaven.

Scriptural Thought:

"Amen, I say to you, today you will be with me in Paradise."

Biblical Story:

The conversion and salvation of a criminal in Luke 23:39–43

DAY 38

Gratitude

My vacation came at a very difficult time last year. At the beginning of it, a doctor called confirming that I had a rare blood cancer, treatable, but incurable. The symptoms of the disease were by then intense: extreme fatigue, an incessant cough, night sweats, and frequent chills. I wept at times and anxiously wondered about my future. Now, eight treatments and only twelve months later, thanks to skilled physicians, potent medicine, much love, and many prayers, those symptoms have disappeared and the cancer is dormant, at least for the present.

On vacation last year, I could barely run a single mile; on vacation this year, I jogged without strain my usual five miles. Such a remarkable recovery has filled me with deep gratitude, grateful to God and to all those others who brought this about, a gratefulness I would not have experienced without the sickness.

Spiritual Suggestion:

Recovery of one's health can and should prompt our intense gratitude to God and others.

Scriptural Thought:

"I love you, Lord, my strength, Lord, my rock, my fortress, my deliverer."

Biblical Story:

King David sings a song of thanksgiving for victory in Psalm 18

Growing Old and Still Productive

For many years Doc Severinsen bantered with Johnny Carson and played his masterful trumpet on *The Tonight Show*. Now seventy-five, Severinsen lives on a ranch one hundred miles north of Los Angeles and cares for the animals on his farm. However, he still practices music at least three and sometimes five hours everyday in a studio near his house. Why such a disciplined life at seventy-five?

Severinsen notes: "The main reason I'm doing all of that practice is I still love to go out and play for people. On the day that stops, then it's over. That's when I quit." And people love to see his colorful outfits and hear his remarkable playing. Two sellout crowds at the Syracuse Symphony Pops Concert gave him repeated standing ovations and still wanted more. By continuing to use his talents, Severinsen has not lost them. Growing older, he is still very productive.

Spiritual Suggestion:

Musician Doc Severinsen demonstrates in his own life how we can continue to grow and still be productive.

Scriptural Thought:

"Well done, my good and faithful servant. . . . Come, share your master's joy."

Biblical Story:

Parable of the ten talents in Matthew 25:1–13

DAY 40

God's Forgiveness

The missionary preacher spoke about God's healing and forgiveness. He said that to have God heal our sickness is a wonderful, but only temporary, blessing because eventually we will die. The preacher reminded us that, on the other hand, when God forgives our sins the forgiveness is everlasting. The missionary used a computer to illustrate his point.

When a hard drive crashes, we can lose everything. Pressing the restart button then gives us a clean slate, a fresh beginning, a screen with no carryover from the past. Through the prophet Isaiah, we hear the preacher's point: The Lord says: "It is I . . . .who wipe out your offenses; your sins I remember no more" (Isaiah 43: 25). That is a very comforting thought for us all.

Spiritual Suggestion:

God's forgiveness is everlasting.

Scriptural Thought:

"There will be more joy in heaven over one sinner who repents than over ninety-nine righteous people who have no need of repentance."

Biblical Story:

Parable of the lost sheep in Luke 15:1–7

God's Nudges

Many years of swimming in the sun are catching up with me. A dermatologist has removed several spots from my face, scalp and back.

But recently an ugly head sore appeared and persisted. A family physician suggested various solutions, but the condition did not improve. Finally, I felt an inner nudge to contact the skin doctor. My physician simultaneously suggested the same.

The specialist performed a biopsy that revealed a cancerous growth. Because of its location, he referred me to a plastic surgeon. There were no immediate openings. However, a week later, I felt another nudge, this time to ask for a place on the cancellation list. An opening appeared and the surgeon successfully excised the cancer, but found it was more aggressive than he first thought. Getting it removed sooner, he said, was a wise move.

Spiritual Suggestion:

It seems that God, while respecting our freedom, sometimes nudges us toward an action that is for our best.

Scriptural Thought:

"Speak, Lord, for your servant is listening."

Biblical Story:

Samuel and Eli in 1 Samuel 3

Day 42

A Vocation to Serve

Peter grew up in a comfortable New England home. After graduating from college, he went on to law school in New York before moving to Syracuse, the home city of his future wife. He spent a few years working in the District Attorney's office, then joined a prestigious local law firm. Peter also married his long-time sweetheart and was looking forward to the birth of their first child.

However, throughout most of his life this fine, bright, young man dreamed of joining the FBI. When the Bureau publicized some openings, Peter applied, was accepted, and began training. Following that inner call cost him.

Peter took a major cut in salary and had to be away during much of his wife's pregnancy. In addition, the first assignment required Peter and his wife to leave family and friends in Syracuse for a new location. Why would he and his wife make such sacrifices? Peter felt a deep call from God to serve others in this fashion. His wife believed in and supported him in that calling, and so the young family took that leap of faith.

Spiritual Suggestion:

God sometimes summons us to serve others in unique ways.

Scriptural Thought:

"When they brought their boats to shore, they left everything and followed him."

Biblical Story:

The call of Peter and others in Luke 5:1–11

Words of Peace for a World at War

In recent years we have experienced a world at war, including sharp conflicts between Christian, Jewish and Muslim peoples. Understanding and respecting the spiritual values we share in common could lessen those dangerous tensions.

One such example is our common reverence for the holy city of Jerusalem. On Friday some years ago, that city witnessed three quite different religious experiences: Christians walked the "via dolorosa" or sorrowful journey Christ made to Calvary on the day of his crucifixion. Jewish people, celebrating the end of Hanukkah at sunset, joined rabbis lighting six candles at the Western Wall. Two hundred thousand Muslims ended Ramadan by turning east at noon and bending to the ground in prayer.

Here is a path to peace: rejoicing in our unity and respecting our differences.

Spiritual Suggestion:

> Christian, Jews, and Muslims share many spiritual beliefs and practices in common.

Scriptural Thought:

> *"I will make of you a great nation, and I will bless you; I will make your name great, so that you will be a blessing."*

Biblical Story:

> Abram's call and migration in Genesis 12

Day 44

Feeding the Hungry and Clothing the Naked

In *The Pianist*, an the Academy Award winning movie, the film's central figure, a Polish Jew and gifted musician, survives the terrible persecution of the Nazis during World War II. The real hero in this true story, however, is the German officer who, in a dramatic sequence at the end, saves the pianist's life.

He discovers the artist hiding in an attic, but neither shoots him on the spot nor turns him over to others for execution. Instead, he secretly brings food to the pianist at his hiding place on several different occasions. Finally, with the Russians about to overtake the Germans in Poland, the officer takes off his coat, tosses it to the shivering pianist, and leaves.

The credits describe the destiny of both after the war. The pianist resumes his career and plays until his death at eighty-eight. The commander dies in a Russian prisoner of war camp.

Spiritual Suggestion:

Do I feed the hungry and clothe the naked on a regular basis?

Scriptural Thought:

"When hunger came to be felt throughout the land of Egypt and the people cried to Pharaoh for bread, Pharaoh directed all Egyptians to go to Joseph and do whatever he told them."

Biblical Story:

Joseph is sold into Egypt and his early days
there in Genesis 37–41

Day 45

Pictures of Reconciliation and Peace

"A picture," the saying goes, "is worth a thousand words." Two contemporary photos, viewed worldwide, capture moving scenes of reconciliation and give hope for peace in our world. They can also inspire us to work equally hard at forgiveness.

In the first photo, a white robed figure sits before a prisoner in a Roman jail holding the incarcerated person's hands. The figure is Pope John Paul II, and that prisoner, the man who only months earlier had attempted to assassinate him. In the second, three men are sitting around a table in Aqaba, Jordan: President Bush, Israeli Prime Minister Sharon, and Palestinian Prime Minister Abbas. "First Signs of Peace" was the headline over this photo. The companion article quoted George Bush: "These first signs of peace happen when people make up their minds to work towards peace."

Spiritual Suggestion:

Two contemporary photos seen worldwide strengthen our hope for universal reconciliation and peace.

Scriptural Thought:

"Peace be with you."

Biblical Story:

Jesus appears to his disciples in John 20:19–23

Practice Makes Perfect

During high school, Gerry McNamara regularly remained in the gym for two hours after his basketball team's weekday workouts. His dad joined him there as this future Syracuse University star practiced foul shots for long stretches of time. Gerry's father returned the ball after each attempt. That sustained effort paid great dividends for McNamara as a freshman on the national championship team. He led the Big East Conference in foul shooting accuracy and his success at the free throw line helped the Orangemen to many victories. Coaches describe him as an awesome person as well as an exceptionally conscientious and dedicated athlete.

Spiritual Suggestion:

Hard work pays off.

Scriptural Thought:

"By the sweat of your face shall you get bread to eat . . . "

Biblical Story:

The sin of our ancestors and its consequences in Genesis 3

Lessons from Brownout 2003

During and after Brownout 2003, many of us in the northeastern United States realized how dependent we are upon electricity, how we usually take this for granted, and how seldom we are truly grateful for it. Christian, Jewish, and Muslim theology and practice would concur that those realizations too often apply to our relationship with God as well. The lessons of Brownout 2003 can continue to serve as a spiritual wake up call for many.

- Muslims are expected to praise God, Allah, the Beneficent One with gratitude many times during the day.
- Devout Jews seek to bless or thank God at least one hundred times daily.
- Christians are called to give thanks always and are reminded of the ten lepers who were healed, with only one returning to give thanks to God.

Spiritual Suggestion:

Do I take God and God's gifts for granted and fail to express my gratitude?

Scriptural Thought:

"Ten were cleansed, were they not? Where are the other nine? Has none but this foreigner returned to give thanks to God?"

Biblical Story:

The cleansing of the ten lepers in Luke 17:11–19

Surrendering to God

I was traveling on a large airbus when a flight attendant tapped my shoulder and said: "You seemed to be reading your Bible. Four of us are having an argument back in the galley, would you come back and help us?" These attendants, one Catholic and the others Protestant, were discussing this question: "Will we be with and recognize in heaven those we have loved on earth?" This was a real concern for them because one's mother had just died and another had lost his five-year-old daughter to cancer.

That father had pleaded constantly with God to spare his daughter's life during her illness. When he finally let go, simply placing his daughter in the Lord's hands, a great peace immediately came over him. His child died quietly thirty minutes later. He believes and looks forward to a time when he will be reunited with his little girl in heaven.

Surrendering our lives to God in various situations can dissolve personal anxieties and bring us peace.

Spiritual Suggestion:

I need to work on surrendering my life to God.

Scriptural Thought:

"By waiting and by calm you shall be saved, in quiet and in trust your strength lies."

Biblical Story:

A futile alliance with Egypt in Isaiah 30

Quiet and Hidden Acts of Charity

Oliver's young wife and the mother of his four children—the oldest of whom was eleven—had been experiencing serious discomfort for several months. However, she resisted her husband's repeated urgings to see a doctor.

Eventually the woman did so, only to discover a huge growth and a cancer that now had spread throughout her body. For the next six months, Oliver, a veteran firefighter, was his spouse's full-time, stay-at-home caregiver. Although he didn't spend a day at work during that time, his paychecks continued.

Did the city, in a gesture of kindness, simply maintain his salary? No. Oliver's firefighting colleagues covered his hours. On their own, despite his protests, they worked extra so he could care for his wife and the children. After her death, Oliver wanted to pay back those weeks of service. His colleagues would not even discuss that possibility.

Many such quiet and hidden acts of charity happen in our midst each day.

Spiritual Suggestion:

The many quiet and hidden acts of charity we hear about can inspire us to do likewise.

Scriptural Thought:

"I was hungry and you gave me food, I was thirsty and you gave me drink, a stranger and you

welcomed me, naked and you clothed me, ill and
you cared for me, in prison and you visited me."

Biblical Story:
The last judgment in Matthew 25:31–46

DAY 50

Ten Commandments

Jazz pianist and composer Dave Brubeck long ago wrote a still popular piece called "Take Five." During World War II, his career and his life almost ended at the month-long Battle of the Bulge in which 19,000 Americans perished, many frozen to death, and 25,000 were captured. Through a combination of factors, he survived that horrible ordeal.

Now eighty-four and married for sixty years, he continues to compose, often religious music. Today's global situation and memories of those earlier deaths prompted him to write some music about the Ten Commandments.

Brubeck maintains that Christian, Jewish, and Muslim people believe in Moses and the commandments he taught, especially "Thou shall not kill." "I've written this piece," he says, "for the specific purpose of bringing them together."

Spiritual Suggestion:

Pray that the Ten Commandments will bring Christians, Jewish and Muslim people together.

Scriptural Thought:

"As Moses came down from Mount Sinai with the two tablets of the commandments in his hands, he did not know that the skin of his face had become radiant while he conversed with the Lord."

Biblical Story:

Moses and the commandments in Exodus 34

The Evil of Satan and the Goodness of God

The Metropolitan Opera's recent extraordinary performance of *Faust* at New York's Lincoln Center powerfully dramatized the evil of Satan. Marguerite, the female lead, is warned not to favor her lover with kisses until she wears his wedding ring. She doesn't heed this advice and as a result gives birth to an illegitimate child. Later, in a deranged moment, she kills the infant. As Marguerite faces life's end, both her brother and Satan curse and condemn the woman.

She, however, turns to God for forgiveness. In the Opera's finale, Marguerite walks between two angels toward a beautiful place of light as the chorus sings: "He has risen."

Spiritual Suggestion:

A work of art, like the opera *Faust*, underscores for us the real evil of Satan and the greater goodness of God.

Scriptural Thought:

"There will be rejoicing among the angels of God over one sinner who repents."

Biblical Story:

The parable of the lost coin in Luke 15:8–10

DAY 52

Friendships

A few years ago in her book *Necessary Losses*, Judith Viorst argued that to grow we must give up certain myths. One of these clings to the notion that we can develop and maintain perfect relationships. The harsh fact is that there are none in this life. Every one of us is a flawed human being and so there are no perfect friendships, work arrangements, or even marriages.

Although all relationships are flawed, most do give us at least some measure of joy. They also can reflect for us (and those around us) the profound joy of a relationship with God. Both the complexity of human relationships and our own flawed nature likewise remind us that God is the one absolutely true friend. God alone totally understands us, loves us unconditionally, and never abandons us.

Spiritual Suggestion:

Friendships are rewarding, but all are flawed. Only God loves perfectly.

Scriptural Thought:

"Let there be no strife between you and me, or between your herdsmen and mine, for we are kinsmen."

Biblical Story:

Abram resolves a conflict with Lot in Genesis 13

Gratitude

During a trip this spring, I came upon a cluster of several hundred tall trees and, drawing nearer, noticed something odd about them. Each one had two or three silver pails attached to its trunk. Then the answer dawned on me: The trees were being tapped for sap. The owners would collect and combine the sap, boil it for the correct period of time and then make maple syrup for pancakes, waffles, and other good things.

After passing the trees and pondering the sight, I thought to myself, "Here is another reason for giving thanks to God." I am grateful to the Creator for the sap-bearing trees as well as for the sun and rain that keep them producing.

And I am grateful to God who has given human beings the ability to harvest the sap and produce the syrup.

Spiritual Suggestion:

We need to be grateful for God's many gifts, both the gifts of nature and the talents of human beings.

Scriptural Thought:

"The Lord God then took the man and settled him in the Garden of Eden, to cultivate and care for it."

Biblical Story:

The second story of creation in Genesis 2:4–25

DAY 54

Loving Each Other

In the distant past, Omar Sharif played a leading role in the classic film *Dr. Zhivago.* He stopped making movies a few years ago but recently reappeared in *Monsieur Ibrahim.* In this film, Sharif plays an Arab grocer who befriends a Jewish boy. Asked why he emerged from semi-retirement to do a new movie, the actor replied: "I thought I should make a statement as a popular person in the Arab world. I wanted to say, look, it is possible to . . . love each other." That kind of statement surely is needed today.

As we have pointed out before, Christians, Jews, and Muslims have many beliefs and practices in common. To love each other means celebrating those areas in which we agree, while understanding and accepting those areas in which we don't.

Spiritual Suggestion:

For peace in the world, people of all faiths and none need to understand, accept, and love one another.

Scriptural Thought:

"Look up at the sky and count the stars, if you can. Just so . . . shall your descendents be."

Biblical Story:

God's covenant with Abram in Genesis 15

The Unfolding of Our Lives

Actress and singer Shirley Jones grew up in a small Pennsylvania town, studied music from age twelve, and was a beauty contestant after graduating from high school. Then, at the age of eighteen, she headed to college hoping to become a veterinarian. Stopping in New York City en route to school, a pianist friend there suggested that, just for the fun of it, Jones sing a few songs at an open audition for the chorus of *South Pacific*. She agreed. Rogers and Hammerstein were impressed, placed her in the show, and, within a year, took Shirley Jones to Hollywood for a star role in the film *Oklahoma*.

Now sixty-nine, this very distinguished lady still performs and draws large, enthusiastic, standing-ovation crowds. Her life unfolded quite differently from what she planned: fifty years, not as a veterinarian, but as an acclaimed musician and actress. I wonder if Shirley Jones sees God's hand in that New York City audition.

Spiritual Suggestion:

We need to be open to a similar positive unfolding of our lives under God's loving care.

Scriptural Thought:

"We know that all things work for good for those who love God . . . "

Biblical Story:

God's indomitable love for us in Romans 8:28–39

DAY 56

Wealthy People Reaching Out to Those in Need

Most, or at least many, of the people in Vero Beach on Florida's East Coast are retired and quite wealthy. But they also seem very willing to share their abundance with those in need.

One day in the parking lot of Holy Cross Catholic parish there, I saw an expensive SUV and a Cadillac with this request printed on homemade signs: "New blankets needed. Place them inside the cars." That is one family's project: supplying a homeless shelter with needed blankets. The parish frequently takes up second collections to fund Habitat for Humanity homes. Over the past decade, they have built fifty of these houses. Once a month church members come to Sunday services with bags of food for people in need. It takes two pickup trucks to transport all of these donated foodstuffs to a local soup kitchen. These parishioners clearly have taken to heart the Gospel message "Whatever you do to the least of my brothers or sisters, you do to me" (Mt 25).

Spiritual Suggestion:

Keep in mind the biblical statement: "It is more blessed to give than to receive" (Acts 20: 35).

Scriptural Thought:

"I am your brother Joseph, whom you once sold into Egypt. But now do not be distressed, and do not reproach yourselves for having sold me here.

It was really for the sake of saving lives that God sent me here ahead of you."

𝓑*iblical* 𝒮*tory:*

Joseph and his brothers reunited in Genesis 42–45

The Footprints of God in Nature

I recently spent a few days in a warmer place by the ocean. As always, both the sea and the sky are, for me, footprints of God. Listening to the constant pounding of huge waves upon the shore or diving through them while swimming gives me an experience of God's power. Nature's laws governing oceans and stars speak to me of God's wisdom and harmony. It is those seemingly timeless patterns that have enabled us to calculate the exact moments of low and high tides. They have also led us to the moon, to other planets, and to the far reaches of our solar system. As I gaze at a far distant horizon or clear blue sky, my mind and heart marvel at the utter beauty and awesomeness of God.

Spiritual Suggestion:

I can seek God's power, wisdom, and awesomeness in the created world that surrounds me.

Scriptural Thought:

"Blessed are you, and praiseworthy, O Lord, the God of our fathers, and glorious forever is your name."

Biblical Story:

Three young men in the fiery furnace of Daniel 3

One Nation under God

During the current debate about the Pledge of Allegiance
and its phrase "One nation under God," I find it interest-
ing to study the attitude of our country's founders and
leaders on this topic.

1. A recent, popular biography of John Adams por-
   trayed him as a very religious and prayerful man.
2. George Washington in his inaugural address called
   upon all nations to recognize the sovereignty of God.
3. Benjamin Franklin once made a simple affirmation:
   "I believe there is one Supreme most perfect being."
4. President Abraham Lincoln, dedicating the
   Gettysburg cemetery after that terrible battle, gave a
   two-minute speech concluding with these words:
   "This nation, under God, shall have a new birth of
   freedom and that the government of the people, by
   the people, for the people, shall not perish from the
   earth!"

Spiritual Suggestion:

It is good to remind ourselves that founders of
the United States were strong believers in God,
as have been many or most of our presidents.

Scriptural Thought:

*"I call with all my heart, O Lord; answer me that
I may observe your laws . . . " " I rise before dawn
and cry out; I put my hope in your words."*

Biblical Story:

A prayer to God the lawgiver from Psalm 119

Time and Eternity

After a wonderful surprise seventieth birthday party, I drove home alone, or rather almost floated back to my residence, quite overwhelmed by this unexpected outpouring of love. The next morning, I followed my custom and spent a lengthy period in reflective prayer, posing these questions to myself: "Since seven decades of my time on earth have passed, what does the next decade hold for me? Will I still be here, or in eternity?"

A partial answer came within a year. I was diagnosed with a rare form of bone marrow cancer, a treatable, but incurable disease. While I was struggling with the symptoms of the cancer and undergoing yearlong treatment, I rather automatically pondered the issue of time here and the eternity to come.

Spiritual Suggestion:

An encounter with a potentially terminal illness makes you appreciate your time here and think a bit about eternity.

Scriptural Thought:

"Then he had a dream: a stairway rested on the ground, with its top reaching to the heavens; and God's messengers were going up and down on it."

Biblical Story:

Jacob's dream at Bethel in Genesis 28:10–22

Respecting Differences

The men's restroom at Radio City Music Hall in New York has a diaper-changing table for fathers bringing their little children to performances.

A printed warning on the device, however, sternly directs all users that a child should never be left unattended. This admonition is printed in several languages: English, Italian, Spanish, and French as well as with those familiar line figures of Japanese. A small square replica of the flag for each originating nation precedes every caution.

That multilingual warning is merely another sign of the global nature of today's society. It also reminds us of our need to understand and respect the great differences among people in our modern world.

Spiritual Suggestion:

Am I comfortable with different people in our modern world?

Scriptural Thought:

"That is why it was called Babel, because there the Lord confused the speech of all the world."

Biblical Story:

The Tower of Babel in Genesis 11:1–9

DAY 61

Divine Impulses and Providential Coincidences

Mary has endured enormous bodily pain from a variety of causes for a half century, ever since she was a teenager. In recent months, the acute difficulty of climbing stairs, getting in and out of cars, or simply walking around has kept her housebound. The local pastor heard about her status and said to himself: "I need to go over to their house and visit Mary."

Two weeks later, he made that call. They chatted for some time and then the priest ministered the comforting ritual of the church for one who is seriously ill. The very next morning, Mary had a massive heart attack. Hospital personnel had to use a defibrillator to revive her. Was the remarkable timing of that priest's positive visit a fluke, some accidental coincidence, or had he received a subtle divine impulse and the coincidence, a sign of God's loving presence?

Spiritual Suggestion:

Faith enables us to detect God's loving presence in routine as well as remarkable coincidences.

Scriptural Thought:

"Show us, Lord, your love; grant us your salvation."

Biblical Story:

A Prayer for Divine Favor in Psalm 85

Dealing with Addictions

Vin Baker is a tall, husky, four-time All-Star professional basketball player. But he also struggles with alcoholism. That disease, and giving in to it, caused the Boston Celtics to terminate his contract with over two years left and $35 million remaining on it. The New York Knicks agreed to give him another chance, partially because their president had a brother die of alcoholism and their owner also battles the disease.

Baker says: "God has blessed me with another opportunity in my career. Being a God-fearing person, I know God won't continue to give me these opportunities." He goes to AA meetings every day, calls his sponsor twice daily and will be tested for alcohol three times a week. But Baker knows that only a higher Power, God, will give him the help he needs to manage this disease. Baker's mother adds: "His life is basketball and going to church."

Spiritual Suggestion:

> Do I struggle with any addictions? Am I willing to admit my disease and seek help to manage it?

Scriptural Thought:

> *"My grace is sufficient for you, for power is made perfect in weakness."*

Biblical Story:

> Paul describes the revelation he received and his own human weakness in 2 Corinthians 12:1–10

DAY 63

A Story of Self-Giving Love

Time magazine's 2004 cover story, featuring the American soldier as "Person of the Year," includes this moving incident describing several acts of self-giving love.

A young soldier in Iraq lost both of his forearms to one of those terrible bombs. The Bible says there is no greater love than to lay down one's life for another—or to give up both of one's forearms. As a nurse was walking the wounded fellow, he turned to her and said: "I don't know what I am going to do. I am supposed to be married when I get home. How am I to wear the ring?"

The nurse, touched deeply by his anguish, held the soldier tight and wisely responded: "You can wear it on a chain around your neck. It will be even closer to your heart."

Spiritual Suggestion:

> This story of a soldier, a nurse, and a wedding ring provides different examples of self-giving love.

Scriptural Thought:

> *"So faith, hope, love remain, these three; but the greatest of these is love."*

Biblical Story:

> A familiar and classic description of love in 1 Corinthians 12:31–13:13

A Spiritual and Prayerful President

We often learn of some unknown qualities about a person upon his or her death. That was the case for me with the late President Ronald Reagan. He was both very spiritual and prayerful. He believed that God had a plan for each of us and that we might not know what it is now, but eventually we will. He always whispered a silent prayer in a plane both when taking off and upon landing. He was an eternal optimist, seeing the glass always half full, not half empty. He prayed for himself and for his "would-be" assassin as he lay in the hospital bed recovering from the bullet wound.

When he was diagnosed with Alzheimer's disease, he wrote this public letter: "I intend to live the remainder of the years God gives me on earth doing the things I have always done . . . When the Lord calls me home, whenever that day may be, I will leave with the greatest love for this country of ours, and eternal optimism for its future."

Spiritual Suggestion:

Praying frequently each day can help us discover God's plan and surrender ourselves to it.

Scriptural Thought:

"Blessed are you, O Lord, merciful God! Forever blessed and honored in your holy name; may all your works forever bless you."

Biblical Story:

Tobit and Sarah's prayers in adversity in Tobit 3

DAY 65

Divine and Human Collaboration

On the western shore of Lake Ontario, between Niagara Falls and Toronto, several miles inland, there are large groves of cultivated fruit trees. The older trees have the grass surrounding them neatly mowed. Younger ones are being carefully nurtured and tender seedlings receive the greatest attention. In a few months, the mature trees will be bearing various kinds of fruit, products of divine and human collaboration.

Human beings work hard to plant and nurture, sustain and harvest these fruit trees. But without the divinely given sun, warmth and water, little fruit would be forthcoming. Isn't that true of all our labors in this world?

Spiritual Suggestion:

Everything I do or accomplish is a collaborative venture involving God and myself.

Scriptural Thought:

"I will now rain down bread from heaven for you. Each day the people are to go out and gather their daily portion."

Biblical Story:

The manna from heaven in Exodus 16

Too Swift Judgment of Others

At our Cathedral we often deal with so-called "street people." Some may be rude, demanding, and at least slightly dishonest. Those few can make us a bit on our guard. A man recently stopped at the parish office. His presence made the female receptionist uneasy. He was looking for a priest whose office is at another location. She sent him there, but he soon returned and said no one was answering the door at that location.

The receptionist then remembered that the priest was on vacation. Despite this information, the man hung around, anxious to talk. I talked to the man and told him the priest was away and wouldn't be back for a week. The man simply said: "I found his wallet."

Bingo! I knew that someone had stolen the priest's wallet a week earlier. This man found it on the street ten blocks away, saw the license identification, and was returning it. He had performed a noble deed, and we had too quickly made a false judgment about the man.

Spiritual Suggestion:

> All of us seem to possess the tendency to make too swift judgments about others.

Scriptural Thought:

> *"Am I my brothers keeper?"*

Biblical Story:

> Cain and Abel in Genesis 4:1–16

DAY 67

The Price of Freedom

A sign outside the Veterans Hospital in Syracuse identifies that building as a medical center and carries this message:

"The price of freedom can be seen here."

A military chaplain who ministers at a German hospital that receives the wounded from Iraq sees that message demonstrated daily. He comforts soldiers without legs or arms or eyes. The Bible says there is no greater love than to lay down one's life for another. That may mean giving up one's time, health, or life itself.

While we may strongly oppose war in general or a conflict in particular, we still need to extend love, prayers, and comfort to our troops willing to lay down their lives and for their loved ones.

Spiritual Suggestion:

Hospitals caring for soldiers wounded in action are reminders of the price paid for our freedom.

Scriptural Thought:

"If it is possible, let this cup pass from me; yet, not as I will, but as you will."

Biblical Story:

Agony in the Garden of Gethsemane in Matthew 26:36–46

Merging the Eternal and the Temporal

The Catholic priest from Puerto Rico, now living in Yonkers, is a physicist and teacher, a columnist for *The New York Times,* and author of a recent book called *God at the Ritz*. He believes that one of the greatest dangers in today's world is the tendency to split or separate the eternal and the temporal, the other world and this world, the life beyond us and life here and now.

The eternal, this man argues, nourishes the temporal; the temporal leads to the eternal. Only the eternal—God—can totally satisfy our human hearts. But the temporal, for example, the beauty of nature, can point us to God. It takes faith to merge these two—the eternal and temporal.

Spiritual Suggestion:

Splitting the eternal and temporal has negative consequences for me. But if I seek to merge the two, I experience positive results.

Scriptural Thought:

"They ate their meals with exultation and sincerity of heart, praising God and enjoying favor with all the people."

Biblical Story:

Description of the Christian community in Acts 2:42–47

DAY 69

Surprising Blessings

Emory Austin is a former TV talk show host, an author, and a breast cancer survivor. This woman is also a very entertaining and inspirational keynote speaker. When 300 people gathered recently for an annual fundraising luncheon that supports a breast cancer foundation, Austin told them her story.

A decade or more ago, Austin awoke from surgery only to hear from her husband three shocking words: "It is malignant." She screamed in anguish and fear. But now, Austin counts cancer as one of the great blessings in her life.

Through the tough treatments and afterwards, Austin found herself becoming more compassionate and more concerned about relationships. She also became acutely conscious of how precious is every moment of life.

Spiritual Suggestion:

As cancer survivors often find that the disease has been a blessing in disguise, so I may find a blessing in my burdens.

Scriptural Thought:

"Fear not! Stand your ground, and you will see the victory the Lord will win for you today."

Biblical Story:

Moses and the Crossing of the Red Sea in Exodus 14–15

Moving on After a Loss

After the death of her husband, a widow slipped into deep depression, withdrew from her social circles, and backed out of her closest relationships. In church at Christmas, she heard from the pulpit a story about another widow. After that woman's husband died, she too cried many tears and likewise crawled into her own shell. But she continued to pray and finally realized that her work on earth was not finished. The woman then began reaching out and subsequently rediscovered joy in her life.

This story so touched the woman in church at Christmas that she went home and immediately reconnected with all her family, friends, and neighbors.

She smiled, laughed, and felt joy for the first time in months.

Spiritual Suggestion:

There comes a time after major loss that we must crawl out of our shell and move on with our lives.

Scriptural Thought:

"Do not be afraid; for behold, I proclaim to you good news of great joy that will be for all the people."

Biblical Story:

An angel and the shepherds in Luke 2:8–14

DAY 71

An Awesome Gift

My treatable but incurable cancer returned. After the public announcement of this relapse, many sent supportive cards or notes. These words from an older, anonymous writer really touched me:

> First, I give thanks to our father in heaven for your priesthood, and for your faithfulness in responding to so great a calling. And now my reason for writing: I want you to know that, with all my heart, and in deep prayer, I have offered God my life for yours. I have asked Our Father to spare you, so that you can continue your great ministry. (I don't presume to think it is a fair exchange.) Now, we must wait and see what he thinks of my poor gift.

The Lord will certainly bless the letter-writer's humility, love, and amazing generosity. But will God demand the donor's life in return for another's extension of a few years? That hardly seems the response of an all-loving Creator.

Spiritual Suggestion:
Am I willing to offer my life for another or accept the other's self-giving love for me?

Scriptural Thought:
"Today the Lord shall deliver you into my hand . . . Thus the whole land shall learn that Israel has a God."

Biblical Story:
David and Goliath in 1 Samuel 17

Nature's Laws and Biblical Teachings

During my growing up days, I learned how to predict the next day's weather. A short song or little jingle gave me that ability. You may also have heard or listened to these verses: "Red skies at night, sailor's delight; red skies in the morning, sailors take warning." In reading my Bible the other day, I noted similar words, but never before made the connection with that jingle.

Responding to his critics, Jesus said: "In the evening you say: 'Tomorrow will be fair, for the sky is red; and in the morning,' 'Today will be stormy, for the sky is red and threatening'" (Mt 16:2–3). Apparently before and at the time of Jesus centuries ago, people knew the same prediction jingle I learned.

Spiritual Suggestion:

The next time I note red skies in the morning or evening, I will think of how Jesus used this phenomenon in his teaching.

Scriptural Thought:

"Why are you terrified? Do you not yet have faith?"

Biblical Story:

The calming of the storm at sea in Mark 4:35–41

DAY 73

Finding God in Everyday Situations

The Trappist monks just south of Rochester, New York, in the Abbey of the Genesee, gather in their chapel for public prayer seven times a day, beginning at two o'clock in the morning. They also often pray at other moments individually and silently. Those reflective periods help them discover God in everyday events.

They find God in their own bodies—marveling at the complexity, harmony, and resiliency. They find God in nature, gazing with wonder at its beauty. They find God in the midst of daily positive events, joyfully grateful over the presence of God in them. Without such reflection, we can easily miss the divine presence in these situations.

Spiritual Suggestion:

> Through prayerful reflection, I can find God in the marvels of my own body, the beauty of nature, and in everyday events.

Scriptural Thought:

> *"Is anything too marvelous for the Lord to do?"*

Biblical Story:

> God promises Abraham that his wife Sarah, even in her old age, will bear a son in Genesis 17–18

Helping Each Other

Recently I flew into Denver's new, huge, and complex airport. An automated train takes you from the gate to other concourses and the terminal. Since this was unfamiliar territory, I felt somewhat confused and a bit uneasy.

I asked a young woman standing next to me on the train if she was from Denver. When she nodded in the affirmative, I sought her help.

One sentence from her gave me all the direction I needed and immediately dissolved my uneasiness. I smiled and thanked her; the woman smiled back and seemed pleased she could help. Helping one another even in simple ways brings joy to the helper and to the one being helped.

Spiritual Suggestion:

Helping one another brings joy to the helper and to the one being helped.

Scriptural Thought:

"It is more blessed to give than to receive."

Biblical Story:

Paul's farewell in Acts 20:17–38

DAY 75

An Answer to Prayer

Kevin had been struggling with an acute form of leukemia for several years. His therapy, often difficult, included two bone marrow transplants, the last one at Buffalo's Roswell Park Cancer Clinic. Recuperation from the transplant there required 130 days residence, with a companion, at a location no more than five minutes from the hospital. The person who had agreed to be with him during this recuperation suddenly could not fulfill that promise.

A distraught Kevin, alone in Buffalo, prayed for help, then telephoned his church over a hundred miles away. Members of that congregation responded immediately and positively. From then on, a different person each day drove the three hours up and back to be with Kevin for a twenty-four hour period. In this, as in most cases, God responded to prayer through others.

Spiritual Suggestion:

God always responds to our prayer, but often in ways we don't expect.

Scriptural Thought:

"Do not be afraid; just have faith."

Biblical Story:

Cure of synagogue official's daughter in Mark 5:21–43

Idealism, Discipline, and Prayer

New England high school senior John Schaeffer was not a likely candidate to sign up for the Marine Corps. He joined because the idea of becoming part of a mission bigger and more important than himself was compelling. He liked looking beyond the individual to a simple ideal. Schaeffer also was unhappy with his own lack of self-discipline and expected the Corps would change that.

Several months at boot camp on Parris Island did. The training also gave him an experience of praying regularly with others not of his tradition. Each night at the scheduled "devotional time," he and a friend knelt on the concrete floor and prayed. Schaefer remarks: "One night I did the prayers from my Greek Orthodox prayer book, the next night it was his turn and we did the Roman Catholic prayers." The young man found idealism, discipline, *and* prayer in the Marine Corps.

Spiritual Suggestion:

Is there a yearning within me for idealism, discipline, and prayer?

Scriptural Thought:

"Do not be afraid . . . because your prayer has been heard."

Biblical Story:

Gabriel announces the birth of John in Luke 1:5–21

Self-Giving

I drove one night to the local mall, my bright yellow Focus filled with five heavy plastic mail containers holding about 2,000 letters. After getting an empty cart from the post office, I wheeled it to my car, opened the trunk, and prepared to transfer those containers to the cart. A tall, heavyset young man nearby saw what I was about, and shouted, "Let me do that for you." He did, enlisting the help of his buddy for the task.

I had never met the lad and even now can't remember his name. But that spontaneous self-giving gesture both aided me with a burdensome task and truly warmed my heart. My guess is that the young man and his colleague felt good about the deed as well. Self-giving does just that: it helps the receiver and brings satisfaction to the giver.

Spiritual Suggestion:

> I need to remind myself that acts of self-giving satisfy a giver's heart and warms the hearts of others.

Scriptural Thought:

> *"You shall love your neighbor as yourself."*

Biblical Story:

> The greatest commandment in Matthew 22:34–40

DAY 78

An Obsession with Winning

The highly successful football coach Vince Lombardi
made famous this phrase: "Winning isn't everything,
it's the only thing." His obsession with winning certainly helped motivate his players to reach down within
themselves for that extra effort. But his preoccupation
with wins caused real losses at home. *When Pride Still
Mattered* is a fine biography about the legendary coach.
It describes his great giftedness in football but also his
glaring weaknesses as a spouse and parent.

His obsession with winning had as unfortunate
consequences in Vince Lombardi's personal life as it
can have in ours. Sportswriter Grantland Rice's well-
known lines form a better philosophy:

> When the one great score comes
> To mark against your name
> He writes not that you won or lost
> But how you played the game

Spiritual Suggestion:

> Has an obsession with winning caused
> unfortunate consequences in my personal or
> family life?

Scriptural Thought:
> *"He must increase; I must decrease."*

Biblical Story:
> John the Baptist speaks about Jesus in John
> 3:22–30

DAY 79

Faith and Prayer

Here are two theological truths: faith is the basis for prayer, and prayer can strengthen our faith. We pray because of faith in a God who responds to our petitions. The Psalms tell us that God hears the cry of the poor, but we also pray to strengthen our sometimes-wavering faith.

The followers of Jesus once pleaded: "Lord, increase our faith."

A religious leader, struggling with his faith, prayed what he called his strange prayer: "Lord, if you exist, make your presence known to me." Faith is the basis for prayer; prayer can strengthen our faith.

Spiritual Suggestion:

Faith enables me to pray; I pray to strengthen my faith.

Scriptural Thought:

"Believe in the Lord Jesus and you and your household will be saved."

Biblical Story:

Paul's deliverance from prison and the salvation of the jailer with his family in Acts 16:25–34

The Joy of Apologizing

During my lecture to priests in Florida, one participant sharply challenged me on a certain point. I was stunned and reacted poorly. Instead of simply listening to that objection and carefully rephrasing it to show my understanding of his comment, I expressed strong disagreement. This inappropriate reaction certainly embarrassed my critic.

Afterward and for the rest of the day, I felt bad about my poor judgment, but did not encounter the man. I did happen to meet him the next night, however. I felt nervous about apologizing, but finally summoned up enough courage and did so. Our visit lifted my burden and filled me with great joy. I am sure the apology brought a similar uplift to my critic.

Spiritual Suggestion:

Apologizing is difficult, but can release a burden and bring us joy.

Scriptural Thought:

"Love your enemies, and pray for those who persecute you."

Biblical Story:

On the love of enemies in Matthew 5:43–48

DAY 81

Following a Call

The Midwestern young man likes and loves his family, the outdoors, and farming. He planned to spend his life following those three passions but a serious accident injuring his eye changed that plan. During the long recuperation, he reflected upon his mortality and began to sense an inner call to the altar. Before the accident, he was a regular weekly churchgoer and prayed daily. That continued afterward, but now he wrestled with this interior summons to become a priest.

The struggle went on for three years. In time the man realized that upon saying "yes" to the inner call, he felt peaceful; upon saying "no" to it, he felt distressed. Eventually, the "yes" won out, and he is, today, a very contented priest, while still loving family, the outdoors, and farming.

Spiritual Suggestion:

> Following the divine call within brings peace; fighting it tends to bring distress.

Scriptural Thought:

> *Moses, however, said to the Lord, "If you please, Lord, I have never been eloquent, neither in the past, nor recently, nor now that you have spoken to your servant; but I am slow of speech and tongue." The Lord said to him . . . "Go then! It is I who will assist you in speaking and teach you what you are to say."*

Biblical Story:

Moses' reluctance and Aaron as his spokesman
in Exodus 4:1–17

DAY 82

Our Unique Gifts

The huge vehicle contained long pipes for transferring fresh concrete from a cement truck to a distant and otherwise inaccessible construction spot. The driver needed to back his massive truck from a very busy avenue, through a narrow gate to its designated location on the building site. I watched him do this from a distant vantagepoint and was surprised to see that he was talking on his cell phone while executing this trucking move.

This truck driver certainly possesses a unique talent for operating such vehicles. I have trouble simply parallel parking my small Ford Focus on a seldom-used street! But he may well feel very uncomfortable and unsure of himself speaking before a large group of people—a task that for me comes easily.

God gives each one of us unique gifts.

Spiritual Suggestion:

What unique gifts has God given me?

Scriptural Thought:

"All good giving and every perfect gift is from above . . ."

Biblical Story:

The value of trials and temptations in James 1:2–18

Meditation

The cover story for *Time*'s August 4, 2003, issue dealt with "The Science of Meditation." A subtitle claims that millions of Americans now meditate for health and well-being. Actress Goldie Hawn, for example, says she has practiced transcendental meditation for thirty-one years, doing so twice a day for at least thirty minutes. Federal Trade Commission lawyers meditate during a daily break on the capitol mall in Washington, DC.

Studies by scholars at the Harvard Medical School indicate that meditating regularly improves one's physical, mental, and emotional health. The *Time* article sketches the history of meditation in Christian, Jewish, and Muslim traditions as well as its practice in other religions. Even if those who meditate do not focus directly on God, they certainly are tapping the divine presence within them during those moments.

Spiritual Suggestion:

> My health and well-being demand that I join the millions of Americans who meditate daily.

Scriptural Thought:

> *"Rising very early before dawn, he left and went off to a deserted place where he prayed."*

Biblical Story:

> Jesus heals and prays in Mark 1:32–42

DAY 84

Weather and Our Moods

One vacation day started overcast, cool, and windy. My mood matched that dark weather. Later, however, the clouds broke open, the warming sun and blue sky appeared, and the wind died down. My mood brightened just as the weather did.

Victor Hugo expresses in his classic novel *Les Miserables* the truth that the weather affects our feelings. He writes that on a serene summer morning, young Marius "was as happy as one always is when the weather is fine." It seemed to Marius "that he had in his heart all the bird songs which he heard, and all the bits of blue sky which he saw through the trees."

Spiritual Suggestion:

I need to be aware of how the weather can affect my moods.

Scriptural Thought:

"Sing to the Lord with thanksgiving; with the lyre celebrate our God, who covers the heavens with clouds, provides rain for the earth . . ."

Biblical Story:

Praise to the Bountiful Lord in Psalm 147

Beauty and Transcendence

Just prior to Christmas more than 1,200 people experienced *The Sixth Annual Winter Solstice* at our cathedral. Most were deeply touched by the beautiful sights and sounds that surrounded them during the two-hour performance. Special lighting enhanced the visual awareness of our century-old church. Very talented musical artists—instrumentalists and vocalists—added their marvelous sounds to the occasion.

Thomas Moore, in his best-selling book, *Care of the Soul,* maintains that beauty arrests us, stops us in our tracks, leads us beyond ourselves. It points people towards transcendence, to the eternal and the timeless. Every human heart longs for just that—the eternal and the timeless. Experiences of beauty like *The Winter Solstice* help us reach that goal.

Spiritual Suggestion:

The beauty in our world can lead us to transcendence, to the eternal and the timeless.

Scriptural Thought:

"*Moses decided: 'I must go over to look at this remarkable sight, and see why the bush is not burned . . . .' God said, 'Come no nearer! Remove the sandals from your feet, for the place where you stand is holy ground.'*"

Biblical Story:

God's call to Moses from the burning bush in Exodus 3

DAY 86

Reaching Out to Others

The young man in his late twenties, even though an accomplished skier, took a chance by going off on his own away from the marked Vermont trail. That decision led to disaster. Badly injured and unconscious after an accident, he was air-lifted to a New England hospital. There he struggled for several days before passing away.

A thousand people tried to comfort his family throughout the calling hours. Moreover, a huge crowd filled the tiny country church, with hundreds standing outside during the funeral. Finally, in an impressive caring gesture, the local volunteer fire department provided a substantial meal for over three hundred people immediately following the service.

When we reach out like that to people in need, we help them, but we also help ourselves.

Spiritual Suggestion:

Remember an occasion when you helped others and yet also felt great satisfaction in doing so.

Scriptural Thought:

"The Lord is my shepherd; there is nothing I lack."

Biblical Story:

A song of David in Psalm 23

Remembering the Happy Times

Broadway star Ted Keegan sang the lead role in *The Phantom of the Opera* more than two thousand times. At a recent Syracuse Symphony Pops Concert, he wowed his audience with the famous song from that musical but also performed a little known tune called "The Happy Times."

The central theme of this song is "I want to remember you remembering the happy times." Memories of happy times bring a smile or a laugh. Keegan cites some of those happy times—the first remembered Christmas, the first time I found a dollar bill in the street or rode a bike down the hill, the first time someone said "I love you."

When we are burdened or feeling down, consciously remembering some of those happy times can in fact change our mood, bring a smile to our face, or even cause us to laugh.

Spiritual Suggestion:

Happy times are moments or signs of God's loving presence in our lives.

Scriptural Thought:

"My son, you are here with me always; everything I have is yours. But now we must celebrate and rejoice, because your brother was dead and has come to life again; he was lost and has been found."

Biblical Story:

Parable of the lost son in Luke 15:11–32

DAY 88

Joy and Sorrow

"Joy is the inevitable result of surrendering ourselves totally to God." So writes a popular author in his book, *God Delights in You.* How do we surrender ourselves totally to God? Striving to be one with God and with those we love is a start. Two things occur when we experience oneness with God and with others: Our joy multiplies, and our sorrow lessens.

Parents know this at the deepest level. Sharing the birth of a child doubles their joy; clinging to one another after the sudden and unexpected death of an infant, softens their sorrow.

We do not achieve perfect oneness with God or with others in this life. But we do experience occasional moments of such oneness, multiplying our joy and lessening our sorrow.

Spiritual Suggestion:

Reflect upon an occasion when being one with God or another increased your joy or eased your sorrow.

Scriptural Thought:

"Blessed be the Lord, the God of Israel."

Biblical Story:

The Canticle of Zechariah in Luke 1:67–80

Regular Church Attendance

How can we be good believers in a world where many do not believe or fail to practice their beliefs? Going to church weekly is one way. The commandment, keep holy the Sabbath, respected by Christian, Jewish, and Muslim peoples, tells us to do that. But there are other benefits to weekly churchgoing besides observing a divine commandment.

At church we are with others who share our most fundamental beliefs and values. It helps us, in the words of one young physician, "to keep grounded, with our focus proper and our priorities correct." We likely find hope and strength at those worship services. Moreover, this weekly practice gives us some moments for quiet reflection and an opportunity to thank God for the other 167 hours we have enjoyed during that past week.

Spiritual Suggestion:

> Going to church regularly can help us be good believers in a world where many do not believe or fail to practice their belief.

Scriptural Thought:

> *"The Lord, my God, has given me peace on all sides. . . . So I propose to build a temple in honor of the Lord, my God . . ."*

Biblical Story:

> Solomon and the building of the temple in 1 Kings 5:15–20

Day 90

Letting Go So We Can Grow

The joy-filled couple holding their tiny first baby had experienced a certain disappointment the night before. The new father recalled with a gesture how at the delivery he had been invited to snip the umbilical cord. They were told that shortly the remains of that cord would dry up, then quite naturally and automatically fall away from the baby's belly button. It did.

Watching this happen made the mother and father a little sad because that cord had been their lifeline to the infant within. It reminded them that they would, in the future, be faced with many such experiences of letting go. If their child were to grow and thrive as a healthy individual, they would need to learn the fine art of letting go gracefully and with some good amount of courage. Parents know at a primal level the awesome power of love that demands of us both constant involvement and constant letting go.

All of us must frequently let go—with trust—if we, and those we love, are to grow.

Spiritual Suggestion:

It is good to recall situations in which the pain of letting go led to great growth.

Scriptural Thought:

"My love, get up. Let us pray and beg our Lord to have mercy on us and to grant us deliverance."

Biblical Story:

The marriage of Tobiah and Sarah in Tobit 7–8

Giving One's Life for Others

In October, the wife, children, relatives, and friends of Baghdad's deputy mayor warned this Iraqi man that he was in grave danger because of his cooperation with Americans. "Why?" he asked, "I am only engineer. But I must follow my heart and continue on." He flew to Madrid and negotiated some excellent economic contracts for the city. Returning home, the elated deputy mayor said that with these arrangements, Baghdad would become like heaven.

Later that evening he walked to a nearby café for relaxation over a game of dominos. Two masked men approached the man, fired five shots into his head and body, and then ran away.

The Bible teaches that there is no greater love then to lay down one's life for others. The deputy mayor hoped to make Baghdad like heaven. I would think that instead he is now in heaven with God.

Spiritual Suggestion:

Such a dark incident of total self-sacrifice stuns, but can and should also inspire.

Scriptural Thought:

"No one has greater love than this, to lay down one's life for one's friends."

Biblical Story:

The vine and the branches in John 15:1–17

Day 92

A Passion for Life

Charlie Weis, Notre Dame's head football coach, walked into a hornets' nest on his first visit to that campus. Many people there and around the nation were angered over the dismissal of the previous coach. Moreover, they were skeptical about this man coming to a college program from the professional ranks. He won them over by the word "nasty" at his initial press conference. Weis said: "Playing with fire, playing with passion, playing like the game is all-important to you, playing as if you dread failure—that's nasty."

Weis believes that "if you don't have a nasty streak in you when you are a competitor, if you don't have that fire inside of you—if you're pinning your chances of being successful solely on ability, without including temperament— then you're not going to win."

To succeed in all of life's activities, we too must have a passion for what we are about.

Spiritual Suggestion:

Do I have a passion for my life's primary work or for the other things that occupy my time?

Scriptural Thought:

"O Lord God, remember me! Strengthen me, O God . . ."

Biblical Story:

Samson and Delilah in Judges 16

A Peacemaker in Death

More people watched the televised funeral of Pope John
Paul II than have watched coverage of any other contemporary event. Leaders of nations around the globe
came to Rome for his burial service. A significant number of them are at odds with each other and some—at
least on the surface—even hostile to one another.

At Roman Catholic Masses, including funerals, participants exchange a sign of peace before the
Communion Rite. This gesture of reconciliation is
meant to empty hearts of hostility and to create a spirit
of oneness prior to approaching the altar for the recep-
tion of communion. It was fascinating to observe those
perhaps alienated leaders turn to each other and speak
the designated greeting: "Peace be with you."

Pope John Paul's ministry of reconciliation seemingly continued even after his death.

Spiritual Suggestion:

Deep inner peace is possible only if we let go of
our hurts whether they are real or only
perceived.

Scriptural Thought:

"Father, forgive them, they know not what they do."

Biblical Story:

Jesus speaks words of forgiveness on the cross
in Luke 23:33–38

Trust in God

People used to think that eagles taught their eaglets to fly like this. The nest was usually located at the edge of a steep cliff overlooking some deep abyss. The eagle pushed the eaglet out of its comfortable nest and over the cliff. The tiny bird swiftly plummeted down, frantically, but without much success, flapping its wings. Just before the eaglet was about to hit a rock bottom, the mother eagle would swoop down, catch the little bird, and return it safely back to the nest. The mature eagles would repeat the process until the eaglet learned how to fly.

God seems to teach us in a similar fashion how to trust: We are pushed out of our comfort zones and allowed to fall or fail on our own. Then, just before disaster, are rescued.

Spiritual Suggestion:

The way eagles train their eaglets to fly can remind us of how God teaches us to trust.

Scriptural Thought:

"Now I know that there is no God in all the earth, except in Israel."

Biblical Story:

Elisha's cure of Naaman the leper in 2 Kings 5

The Challenge of a Change

A change always challenges us, especially in the beginning. I recently began a four-hour drive to Hershey, Pennsylvania. MapQuest recommended a switch at Clark's Summit from Route 81 to the Turnpike. The entrance there is very busy, somewhat complicated, and unfamiliar to me. I nervously drove up to the gate expecting to reach out and receive the usual ticket. Instead, there was no person in the booth, only a receptacle for fifty cents in coins.

I panicked, thinking that I had no change. There was some kind of contraption to take bills and provide coins. But that meant leaving my auto and figuring out the process, thus holding up a dozen cars with impatient drivers. Fortunately, I found two quarters and threw them into the receptacle. On my return, I made sure I had coins available.

The new system must be cost effective, but the change surely challenged some of us—at least in the beginning.

Spiritual Suggestion:

A change, even for the better, usually challenges us at first.

Scriptural Thought:

"Wherever you go I will go, wherever you lodge I will lodge, your people shall be my people, and your God my God."

Biblical Story:

The story of Ruth and Naomi in Ruth 1

DAY 96

Coping with Addiction

Driving down one of our city streets, I noticed a shop owner emptying a bucket of water on something in the gutter in front of his store. Passing by, I saw that it was not something, but someone lying in the gutter, someone I know quite well. The prone figure is a familiar face in the area, a long-time alcoholic, a street person who apparently had a very bad night. That addiction has clouded and crippled much of this man's life.

How can addicts, like this poor fellow, check the disease, bring their lives under control, and make their lives manageable? Recognizing that they have a problem and are powerless over it is the critical first step. The next two steps are:

1) Believing in a power greater than themselves who will help them and
2) Taking advantage of the assistance available.

Spiritual Suggestion:

Recognizing that we have a problem and are powerless before it is the first and essential step in coping with an addiction.

Scriptural Thought:

"My grace is sufficient for you, for power is made perfect in weakness."

Biblical Story:

Paul describes the revelation he received and his own human weakness in 2 Corinthians 12:1–10

Healthcare Proxies

Terri Schiavo's life and death prompted many to think about their own healthcare proxies and living wills—at least for a few months. I did, and soon began developing my own plans aided by close friends, a physician and his wife who is also a nurse. What became immediately clear was the need to discuss the issues involved at length with those dear to me.

Medical care today is complex and continuously changing. A simple statement on a document will not cover the decisions that may need to be made.

Extended discussions will enable those who may have to make end-of-life decisions on my behalf to know what my basic thoughts and attitudes are on such matters. Here is a medical reminder: Developing a healthcare proxy or living will does not hasten your death!

Spiritual Suggestion:

Preparing healthcare proxies or living wills is highly desirable, but should involve extended personal conversations with all people concerned.

Scriptural Thought:

"Therefore, stay awake, for you know neither the day nor the hour."

Biblical Story:

The parable of the Ten Virgins in Matthew in 25:1–13

Day 98

Ritualizing Significant Moments

Timothy Collins' father was a career military man; two of his sons have followed in their grandfather's footsteps, including one who recently graduated from the Naval Academy. Tim himself served both in Vietnam and the Gulf War, then remained active all his life in the reserves, finally retiring as a Colonel. His life ended unexpectedly and suddenly—not in battle but riding a bicycle for recreation. He fell victim to an undetected heart ailment. Soldiers from Fort Drum surrounded his burial at the Veteran's Cemetery with full military ceremony—the twenty-one-gun salute, taps, and a flag folded into a triangle presented to his widow.

These solemn rituals always impress me. They remind us of how we need to treat significant moments in our lives with great care and simple ritual. Common moments in our lives that we do well to ritualize include tucking a child in for the night or kissing someone goodbye when he or she leaves the house.

Spiritual Suggestion:

Recall an occasion when you did or did not treat carefully a significant moment in your life.

Scriptural Thought:

"The kingdom of God is at hand. Repent, and believe in the gospel."

Biblical Story:

Jesus begins his ministry in Mark 1:14–15

A Self-Confident Leader

Few people were impressed with Abraham Lincoln's credentials when he ran for president and was newly elected. He had spent only a single term in Congress, failed to win two Senate races, and completed but one year of formal schooling. Some critics went so far as to say that he was "a third-rate Western lawyer and a fourth-rate lecturer who cannot speak grammar." After his surprising election, however, he displayed deep emotional strength, great courage, and confident self-reliance with his first decision.

Lincoln appointed three powerful political rivals to his cabinet and in time gained their admiration by the way he worked with them. Only a very confident leader can do something like that.

Spiritual Suggestion:

Self-confident leaders are comfortable surrounding themselves with the best and the brightest.

Scriptural Thought:

"My soul proclaims the greatness of the Lord; my spirit rejoices in God my savior."

Biblical Story:

Mary's Magnificat in Luke 1:46–56

DAY 100

Pride, Fear, and Prayer

My friend, in his sixties, went for a dip in the Atlantic Ocean by the Delaware Shore. He is in decent shape and an experienced swimmer but encountered a strong undertow and fierce rip tides. He tried several times to make it to the shore but kept being pulled back out into the ocean. With his strength vanishing, my friend became rather frightened but felt embarrassed to cry for help. Finally, fear overcame his pride and he asked several younger men nearby to help him.

They were there in an instant, escorted him to the shore, and would not let my friend go until he was standing safely on the beach. Here is a great example of our reluctance to ask for help, and a very noble response to someone in need.

Spiritual Suggestion:

Fear can overcome a pride that is reluctant to ask for help, even from God.

Scriptural Thought:

"Ask and you will receive, seek and you will find, knock and the door will be opened to you."

Biblical Story:

Prayers are answered in Luke 11:9–13

Acknowledgments

This book, like *Slow Down*, evolved over a two-year period from sixty-second radio spots. In developing both those messages and these, I am deeply grateful to the following people:

- Paul Cowley of Cowley Associates, who made the initial suggestion about a spiritual message on the radio.

- Mary Dougherty, Account Executive for Clear Channel Communications in Syracuse, who again arranged the time, financial details, and recording schedule.

- David Dominski, production director at Clear Channel, whose commitment to excellence in recording these one hundred spots made them much better.

- Nia Carter, for developing and recording the radio spots tagline.

- Joel Delmonico, Vice President of Clear Channel Radio in Syracuse, for continued support of these spots during turbulent commercial times in the radio industry.

- Stewart Hancock, publisher of Eagle Newspapers, who liked the original radio spots and whose weekly papers continue to publish them.

- Robert Hamma at Ave Maria Press, who saw the possibilities of a book that led to *Slow Down* and, because of its success, immediately agreed to *Take Five* as a sequel to it.

- The marketing staff at Ave Maria Press, who strongly promoted *Slow Down* and swiftly shipped copies in response to urgent requests.

- Eileen M. Ponder, Editor of Pastoral Ministry Resources at Ave Maria Press, for her fine work on my manuscript.

- Denise Head and the Barnes & Noble team, whose very successful Advent signing and massive pre-Christmas sales gave us great encouragement when *Slow Down* first appeared.

- Ann Tyndall, for not only typing the original radio messages but formatting this book on computer. She has been an invaluable consultant all along the way.

- Cathy Schotthoefer, for her help in getting me started in identifying one hundred Biblical stories.

- William, Mary, and Tom (pseudonyms to protect their privacy), whose positive experiences appear in the introduction to this book.

- Bishop Thomas J. Costello, who graciously granted the *Imprimatur*, but, more, whose friendship of over fifty years I treasure and whose gifted editing skill always enhances my manuscripts.

- All the known and unknown persons who over the past three years have praised both the radio spots and *Slow Down*, finding them helpful and thus making very worthwhile the efforts to offer these spiritual suggestions for a stress-filled society.

Resources

Introduction: Dan Brown, *Angels and Demons*
 Newsweek, September 5, 2005

Day 2:   Caroline Kennedy, *A Patriot's Handbook*

Day 3   *Syracuse Post-Standard,* May 5, 2003

Day 6   William Rhoden, *New York Times*, June 2, 2003

Day 7   *USA Today,* June 11-17, 2003

Day 9   Nicholas Sparks, *The Guardian*

Day 13   John and Frank Schaeffer, *Keeping Faith*

Day 19   Doris Kearns Goodwin, *Time,* July 4, 2005

Day 20   *USA Today* November 24, 2004

Day 37   Alice Sebold, *The Lovely Bones*

Day 39   *Syracuse Post-Standard*, January 26, 2003

Day 43   Bruce Feiler, *Abraham*

Day 45   *St. Louis Post-Dispatch*, June 5, 2003

Day 50   *London Tablet,* December 18-25, 2004

Day 52   Judith Viorst, *Necessary Losses*

Day 54   *Time,* December 8, 2003

Day 58   Walter Isaacson, *Benjamin Franklin*; Caroline Kennedy, *A Patriot's Handbook*

Day 62   *USA Today*, March 20, 2004

Day 63   *Time*, December 29, 2003

Day 64   *Time*, December 14, 2004

Day 68   Lorenzo Albacete, *God at the Ritz*

Day 70   John Catoir, *God Delights in You*

Day 76   John and Frank Schaeffer, *Keeping Faith*

Day 78   David Maraniss, *When Pride Still Mattered*

Day 83   *Time*, August 4, 2003

Day 84   Victor Hugo, *Les Miserables*

Day 85   Thomas Moore, *Care of the Soul*

Day 92   *Notre Dame Magazine*, Spring 2005

Day 94   Thomas Keating, *Journey to the Center*

Day 99   Doris Kearns Goodwin, *Team of Rivals: The Political Genius of Abraham Lincoln*

Index of Topics

Number(s) following each entry indicates day(s) the topic occurs.

Father Joseph M. Champlin, former rector at the Cathedral of the Immaculate Conception in his home diocese of Syracuse, is now semi-retired and serves in sacramental ministry at Our Lady of Counsel in Warners, New York.

He has traveled more than two million miles lecturing in the United States and abroad on pastoral subjects. Fr. Champlin has written more than fifty books. His works include *Slow Down* (Sorin Books), *Should We Marry?*, *From the Heart*, *Together for Life*, and *Through Death to Life* (Ave Maria Press).

Also by Joseph M. Champlin

joseph m. champlin

s l o w   d o w n

five-minute meditations to de-stress your days

Slow Down
Five-Minute Meditations to De-Stress Your Days
Now people everywhere can reduce the stress that results from their
never-slow-down days with a little help from Father Champlin. Each
message is accompanied by a spiritual suggestion for reflection and a
prayer taken from the Psalms.
ISBN: 1-893732-78-9 / 208 pages / $9.95